CW01521813

Mathematical Investigations in Your Classroom

Mathematical Investigations in Your Classroom

A guide for teachers

Susan Pirie
Lecturer in Mathematics,
University of Warwick

MACMILLAN
EDUCATION

First published 1987
Reprinted 1987

Published by
MACMILLAN EDUCATION LTD
Houndmills, Basingstoke, Hampshire RG21 2XS
and London
Companies and representatives
throughout the world

Typeset by TecSet Ltd, Wallington, Surrey

Printed in Great Britain by
Vine & Gorfin Ltd, Exmouth, Devon

British Library Cataloguing in Publication Data
Pirie, Susan
Mathematical investigations in your
classroom : a guide for teachers.
1. Mathematics
I. Title
510   QA43
ISBN 0-333-44628-3

Contents

Preface

This book arises out of the project *Changing Methods of Teaching Mathematics* which is based at the Department of Educational Studies, University of Oxford and is supported by IBM.

With the invaluable help of John Backhouse, I ran two DES Regional Courses on 'Investigations and problem solving in secondary schools' which were attended by over fifty teachers. I followed up these courses by working with several individual teachers who were tackling the problem of incorporating investigations into their teaching styles without the support of like-minded colleagues. The guide is based on these experiences and on feedback from the participants. It is intended for individual teachers who want to start doing such work with their pupils, and is produced as a loose-leaf file to enable you to add your own notes, comments, investigation write-ups and lesson plans. It is a working document, not armchair reading! The contents include 64 investigations, each tried out by at least six teachers, and classroom hints for most of these can be found in the relevant appendices. You are invited, however, to expand this collection by adding to Chapter 13 new ideas culled from other sources.

I should like to thank all those teachers who provided me with feedback on the materials and especially Phil, Jude, Brenda and Rita for their help and advice. Thanks must also go to Michael Barber for introducing me to my first investigation and to Rolph Schwarzenberger for criticisms and patient proof-reading. My greatest debt of gratitude, however, is to John Backhouse without whom this work might not have existed.

My hope is that this guide will enable you to enjoy working with investigations and communicate this enjoyment to your pupils.

Have fun!

Introduction

Who is this guide for?

Ever since Cockcroft put 'problem solving and investigational work' into paragraph 243, the number of teachers who readily teach in this way has been steadily growing. So too has the number of teachers who feel they *ought* to be taking investigations into their classrooms, but lack the confidence, knowledge or skills to make this dramatic change in their teaching style. And dramatic change it certainly is, for many whose style is based on exposition, consolidation and practice and who, judged by examination results, have been successful in their teaching. This guide in no way underestimates the difficulties inherent in such change, but it is hoped that the assistance and encouragement which is offered will give you the courage, little by little, to attempt this metamorphosis. If you see yourself represented in some way in this paragraph, then this guide is for you.

Aims

The aims of the guide are two-fold: first, to let you experience the fun and challenge of doing some investigative mathematical thinking *yourself* and secondly to guide and support you as you take these investigations into your classrooms. There are always plenty of reasons for not indulging in an hour's mathematical work unrelated to lesson preparation. The demands of this guide give you the excuse your conscience may need!

This introductory chapter attempts to answer some of the fundamental questions which you may be asking, and then goes on to give an outline of the guide and some hints on how best to study the materials provided.

What is an investigation?

There are probably nearly as many different answers to this question as there are investigators. No fruitful service will be performed by indulging in the 'investigation' versus 'problem-solving' debate. It suffices to say that many processes and skills are common to both activities and throughout the text the word 'investigation' is taken to cover the whole spectrum of open working with the possible exception of 'real-world problem-solving'.

A valid response to the above question is to start by saying what it is *not*. It is not a task with a prescribed route to a single solution. It is not an exercise with the overt intention of repetitiously practising a mathematical skill albeit disguised as a word problem. An investigation presents an open situation. For the pupil there are no known outcomes. There may be no known outcomes at all. Pupils are not expected to produce 'the right answer' but are required to explore possibilities, make conjectures and convince themselves and others of what they find. The emphasis is on exploring a piece of mathematics in all directions. The journey, not the destination, is the goal.

What makes a good investigation?

This question is much harder to answer and will be returned to from time to time throughout the guide. The basic ingredients of open ending and open starting points require that non-trivial results and richness of mathematical exploration are also available. The answer also depends on the reasons why your pupils are engaged in a particular activity, since you may have specific criteria for your choice of investigation, although the way of working is through exploration and imagination.

Why do investigations?

Why have you embarked on this guide? Maybe because you feel some mathematical event is passing you by: you feel you are missing out. Maybe you feel pressured by your head of department, or by your peers. Maybe the threat of first the Cockcroft report and now the criteria for the GCSE weigh on your mind. Be honest with yourself – these are all legitimate reasons for 'giving investigations a try'.

Why should pupils do investigations?

Investigations offer pupils a way to become involved in mathematics-in-the-making. They encourage pupils to engage in mathematical thinking, rather than merely to absorb mathematical thought. Some of the claims that are made for investigations are listed below. They can:

1 promote pupils' enjoyment of mathematics.
2 make mathematical experience accessible to pupils by demystifying its subject matter.
3 restore and develop pupils' faith in their own common sense.
4 give pupils the understanding that, even in a mathematics classroom, opinions and personal ideas are valued.
5 present mathematics, not as an imposing body of knowledge to be digested, but as an activity in which pupils can participate.
6 provide situations where pupil–pupil and pupil–teacher discussions arise naturally.
7 offer variety to the pace and presentation of mathematics lessons.
8 increase pupils' willingness to 'have a go' since the threat of being wrong no longer hangs bleakly over them.
9 enlarge conceptual understanding.
10 raise the teacher's awareness of each pupil's mathematical thinking in a way that no marked exercise can.

It must be said at this juncture that investigations are not a universal panacea for all our mathematics teaching ills. Some may suggest that one's aim should be to eventually teach everything in an enquiring and investigative manner. I do not totally endorse this view. Certainly I feel that not all mathematics should be taught through investigations. There will always be a place for expository teaching. (There will certainly always be a place for consolidation.) Even a diet of rich chocolate cake becomes boring eventually!

Why should investigations not be introduced into the mathematics classroom?

It is easy to extol the virtues of curriculum change and to overlook the very real reasons why the change has not taken place before.

**Introductory Activity
Do it now!**

Before reading on, pause and list the reasons why you have been hesitant to indulge in investigations. This list is important in order to be able to evaluate, at the end of the guide, what you have gained and which of your objections have not been sufficiently countered. Some of the fears and reservations which other teachers have had are listed on page 5, but compile your own personal list before turning to their ideas.

The hope is that you will be enabled by the end of the guide

to have moved from a position of apprehension . . .

to taking a deep breath and jumping into the pool . . .

and then on to mastering the skills and techniques necessary to swim with confidence in the investigational shallows . . .

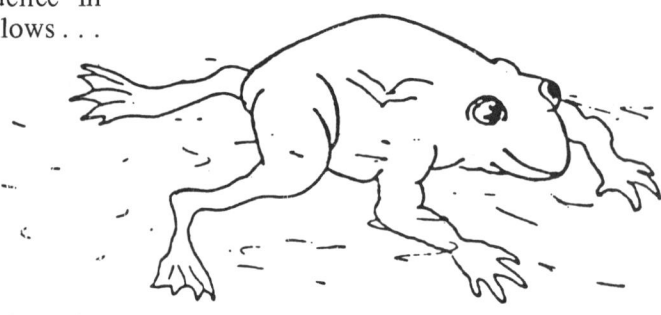

You may even develop the desire to plunge deeper and swim further.

The hope for your pupils is that they will be enabled to engage in real mathematical thinking and to see behind the rules and rote techniques and appreciate a little of the connected complexity and insights which go to building up a deeper understanding of mathematics.

Outline

This book is not intended to be an experience in passive reading and thinking deeply from your armchair. To participate you must be active both in doing the mathematics yourself and in trying the recommended investigations with your classes. If you can persuade one of your colleagues to become involved with the same investigations as you are trying, then the benefit of the feed-back that you can give each other will greatly enhance your learning.

There are four key elements around which the book is built:

1 Your personal experience of *doing* an investigation.
2 Reflection on this experience.
3 Your personal experience of taking the same investigation into a classroom.
4 Reflection on this experience.

In addition the feeling which should pervade the whole enterprise is one of exploration and enjoyment.

Chapter 1 gives you a first investigation to try and leads you through it in such a way that you will be supported in your 'doing' and given guidance as to how to take it into the classroom.

Chapter 2 offers you a choice of investigations to work with unaided and a way of reflecting to advantage on what you have been doing.

Chapter 3 suggests a detailed but adaptable way of planning your investigation for the classroom.

Chapter 4 looks at a model for investigations, indicating the stages and mathematical processes involved.

Chapter 5 considers investigations which are focused on particular aspects of process.

Chapter 6 concentrates attention on class management.

Chapter 7 presents a collection of investigations focused on mathematical topics.

Chapter 8 tackles the twin problems of recording and writing-up.

Chapter 9 illustrates how practical work can also be investigative.

Chapter 10 covers assessment.

Chapter 11 discusses the value of investigations at sixth form level.

Chapter 12 presents you with a collection of '15-minute fillers'.

Chapter 13 is the start of your own collection of investigations.

Appendix to the Introduction

- I shall lose control of whether they are doing worthwhile maths.
- I shall lose control of the class if they talk and wander about.
- It is bound to be noisy and disturb others.
- It will involve too much furniture-shifting and apparatus.
- I have no time because of exam and syllabus pressures, and so
    – it is only for the lower ability range.
    – it is only for first and second year pupils.
- My classes are too large and we have no equivalent of the laboratory technician.
- The pupils won't like it because it 'isn't real maths'.
- My role will be eroded; I won't be teaching them.
- Exposition and practice have always worked for me.
- I may not be able to cope with some of their questions.
- The pupils will be all over the place with their maths.
- How can I know what they have learned?

1   Bogus billiards

Before starting to read this chapter, arm yourself with some squared paper, a sharp pencil and a ruler.

Problem 1.1
Bogus billiards

A ball is hit from one corner of a rectangular table to strike the opposite side at 45 degrees. How many times will it hit the side before falling into one of the corner pockets?

How are you going to get started? An obvious step is to represent the problem in the form of a picture:

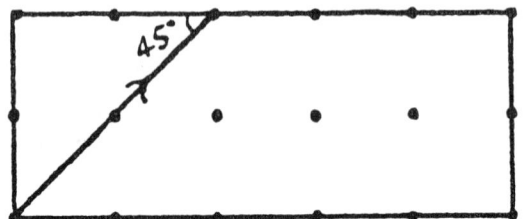

What will happen to the ball on hitting the side? At this stage you need to make some assumptions about smooth spherical balls, frictionless tables and so forth in order to get an initial mathematical model to work with. BUT be aware that this is what you are doing. If one of the aims of doing investigations is to demystify mathematics for pupils, then problems presented in a real-world context must be seen to acknowledge the limitations and complications of the real situation and any assumptions and modelling that occur must be overt. In this case the task is introduced, not so much to model a real-world situation as to use the real world to present pupils with a dynamic image of the problem. 'Let's imagine . . .' can be a good introductory remark.

So, assume that the ball leaves the point of impact at 45 degrees to the side and continues to ricochet off the sides until it falls into one of the corner pockets. You also need to assume that the side pockets do not exist and, for the sake of interest and an open problem, that the table can be of any dimensions not merely the proportions of a real table. The continuation of the problem illustrated above will look something like this:

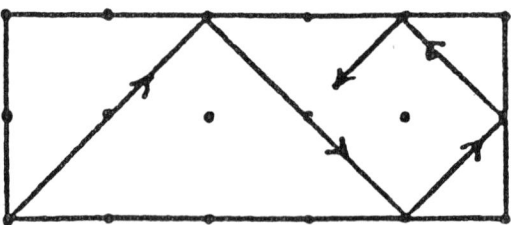

Activity 1.1
Do it now!

Now draw some tables and ball paths and write down the numbers of bounces. (Spend 15 to 20 minutes on this activity.)

Mathematics has been described as a study of patterns and relationships, and certainly if this investigation has any intrinsic interest a first step towards unlocking its secrets is to look for relationships between the numbers that are being generated. Some form of systematic working or recording usually allows patterns to be more readily spotted. A helpful method of combining the results in this case might be to enter the number of bounces into a table with the dimensions of the lengths of the two sides across the top and down the side. However, you might well devise some other representation of your recordings which is helpful to *you*.

<table>
<tr><td>

**Activity 1.2
Do it now!**

</td><td>

Devise some systematic method of recording.
- Look for patterns emerging.
- Can you guess at possible relationships?
- Can you predict the number of bounces on a 2 × 17 table?
- Can you predict the number of bounces on a 12 × 17 table?
- Can you predict the number of bounces on a 12 × 15 table?
- Check your conjectures.
- Could you predict the number of bounces for any table?
- Can you record your conjecture using mathematical, language and symbols?
- Can you prove it?

</td></tr>
</table>

The mathematician Hilbert, at an international congress in Paris in 1900, said in his talk on 'Mathematical Problems':

A mathematical problem should be difficult in order to entice us, yet not completely inaccessible, lest it mock our efforts.

One of the features of a good investigation is that it can be relevant to people of widely differing abilities. In particular it can be extended to offer a challenge to the more able.

<table>
<tr><td>

**Activity 1.3
Do it now!**

</td><td>

Extension: Which pocket will the ball fall into?

</td></tr>
</table>

Further extensions which you might like to try are:
- How many squares will the ball cross?
- What would happen if the angle of impact were not 45°?
- If the ball were hit diagonally across the table into the opposite pocket, how many squares would it go through?
- Return to the initial assumptions that were made. Is there anything of interest to be explored in a situation closer to the real one?

Having spent some fruitful and, it is hoped, enjoyable time 'doing' a piece of mathematics, now consider how it might go in a classroom.

The problem is posed in a clear manner, with a question which immediately gives a point of entry. It is appropriate to any age and ability of pupil and, since it is not specifically related to any mathematical topic on the syllabus, can be injected into the curriculum at any time. You are not being asked at this stage to plan the investigation for a specific class (although if you are feeling brave you might want to), merely to reflect on the way in which the text guided you through your working.

This guided method has some affinity with working on an investigation as a whole class with the teacher acting as a focus for discussion. The structure consists of:

1. An initial public clarification of the problem, and any modelling being used, with possibly a suggestion (in this case drawing on squared paper) of how to get started.
2. Private exploration time – not too long.
3. A coming together of the group to pool initial results and discuss useful ways of recording them.

4 The compilation by the group of some questions on which they might like to focus.
5 Further private exploration time.

Whether the group then reconvenes as a whole at a later time is a decision for the teacher or the participants. In many situations the investigators will be travelling down such divergent paths that attempting to pool ideas again may be irrelevant or positively unhelpful.

Extension questions can always be produced from good investigations to counter the cry of 'I've finished. What can I do now?' This important feature is discussed further in Chapter 4.

For a group of low-ability or young pupils you might like to consider the microcomputer program SNOOK on the Shell/ITMA disc *Some Lessons in Mathematics with a Microcomputer*, which explores a different but related problem in which the patterns are easier to spot.

2 A second investigation

In this and most of the subsequent chapters you will be offered a selection of investigations from which to choose one (or two or three or four) which you are interested in working on. The four investigations given below have been chosen as ones which can be used with any age or ability level. They have also been deliberately worded to illustrate four different methods of presentation.

Problem 2.1
Dots and areas

Draw any straight-sided shape on 'dotty' paper. Is there any connection between its area, the number of dots inside the shape, and the number of dots on the perimeter?

– a question to answer and a direction on how to start.
(*Presentation Method I*)

Problem 2.2
Consecutive sums

Some numbers can be written as the sum of two or more consecutive numbers. Investigate.

– a bald statement which needs to be translated into a problem.
(*Presentation Method II*)

Problem 2.3
S-factors

16 can be written as a sum of smaller numbers in several ways.
For example 16 = 12 + 4   (the product of 12 and 4 is 48)
        or 16 = 5 + 7 + 3 + 1 (the product of 5, 7, 3 and 1 is 105).
Call these smaller numbers S-factors (sum factors). Can you find the set of S-factors for 16 which gives the largest product?

– an explicit question with examples.
(*Presentation Method III*)

Problem 2.4
Right angles in a polygon

Given the number of sides of a polygon, how many right angles can it have?

– a vague question which leaves the investigation wide open.
(*Presentation Method IV*)

Activity 2.1
Do it now!

Choose just one of these four investigations and work at it for at least three-quarters of an hour. You may find that you become obsessed and want to spend much longer than this – three hours, or even three days. Your aim here is to delve deeply into one problem rather than superficially skim all four. Of course if you wish to delve deeply into four problems, good luck to you. Have fun!

While the experience is still fresh in your mind, it is worth spending a little time reflecting on your feelings and actions as you worked through your investigation. This will give you insight into some of the emotions and re-actions you may evoke in your classroom.

Activity 2.2
Do it now!

Think honestly about the following questions:
- How did you feel about getting started?
- Did you put it off?
- What did you do to get started?

- Did you want to ask questions?
- Did you want clarification?
- Were you afraid of being 'wrong'?
- Were you afraid of being mathematically inadequate?
- Did you want reassurance?
- What guidance would you have liked?
- What emotional stages did you go through?
- Did your level of interest change?
- What mathematical stages did you go through?
- What methodological stages did you go through?
- What strategies did you have for working at the problem?

When you have done what you can on the investigation you have chosen, you might like to look at Appendix 2. The way of doing the investigation which is sketched there is not necessarily the best one. There are always many ways in which a good investigation can be tackled. What matters is that you are thinking mathematically in a way that suits you. This is a point you need to have at the back of your mind when you introduce investigations into the classroom (Chapter 3).

Appendix to Chapter 2

Chapter 3 discusses in detail how to prepare yourself to take an investigation into your classroom and page 19 gives some starting suggestions. The classroom notes here, therefore, are specific extra comments.

DOTS AND AREAS

Doing hints   Getting started is easy – draw a shape! You need to decide early on how you will measure area: unit squares? unit triangles? You have three variables: area, inside dots, perimeter dots, and possibly a fourth, shape. Simplify the problem by keeping several of the variables constant. Remember that zero is also a possible constant value! Do *lots* of drawing. Tabulating your results should help you to spot some number patterns. If you think you have a rule, predict, draw and check on a new example. Can you express your rule algebraically? Final hint: for suitable functions $f(x)$ and $g(x)$, of x, the perimeter number = f(area) + g(interior number) + constant. Different ways of measuring the area will result in different functions f and g.

Extensions
  (i)   Try using isometric 'dotty' paper.
  (ii)   Is there a relationship involving the number of sides of a shape?
  (iii)   What about shapes such as these with 'holes'?

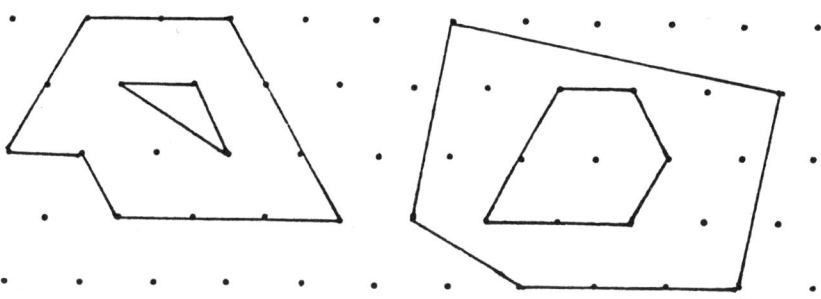

Class presentation hints
Age and ability: Anyone.
Materials: Dotty paper – square or isometric depending on ability of the group.

A word of warning: do not expect algebraic representations from your pupils yet. Let their aim be to spot some patterns and try to explain them to a neighbour – the different functions f and g can provoke stimulating argument!

CONSECUTIVE SUMS

Doing hints   Find some numbers which work, e.g. 6 = 1 + 2 + 3, 17 = 8 + 9, 20 = 2 + 3 + 4 + 5 + 6. Are there some which don't work? There are two main ways of tackling this investigation. You could either start with the numbers 1, 2, 3, . . . and see which can be made up of sums of consecutive numbers, or you could look at sums of consecutive numbers and see what numbers they make, e.g. 1 + 2 = 3, 6 + 7 = 13. Systematic organisation and a clear recording system are essential, whichever route you choose. Don't forget that the sums can be of two or more consecutive numbers. Can some numbers be written in more than one way? Can you predict for any number whether it is a consecutive sum and how to break it down? Can you prove your theory?

Extensions
  (i)   What happens if you include negative numbers?
  (ii)   What about consecutive odd numbers?
  (iii) Investigate numbers formed from the products of consecutive numbers.
  (iv) What happens if you sum the squares of consecutive numbers?

Class presentation hints
Age and ability: Anyone.
Materials: None - or possibly calculators.

Before the class starts be sure they really know what 'consecutive' means. Will you allow 1 + 2 + 3 + 2? Children (and even adults) are not naturally systematic, and you may need to push them gently towards some useful recording system which will help them to spot patterns, but do not interfere with their method of approach.

S-FACTORS

Doing hints   You could set out all the possible decompositions of 16 into S-factors and find the largest product. You would need a careful strategy for ensuring that you had *all* the sets of S-factors. Alternatively you could look at simpler (i.e. smaller) numbers first and see if you could find a pattern which would allow you to predict the set of maximum-product S-factors for any number, not just 16. This second approach is one which is very often a suitable way into an investigation. What happens if the S-factors are not integers?

Class presentation hints
Age and ability: Anyone.
Materials: None – or possibly calculators.

If this is the pupils' first taste of investigations, you will probably need to suggest to those who embark on the first method above, but flounder, that they should try smaller numbers first. This is a good moment to introduce power notation to those who need it. When the pupils think they have found a way of predicting the S-factors for any number, they may enjoy finding the largest number whose S-factor product will fit on their calculator. Sixth formers could put their knowledge of calculus to good use.

Extensions
  (i)   Excluding 1's, which sets of S-factors give minimum products?
  (ii)   For which numbers do there exist sets of S-factors which are also the multiplicative factors?

RIGHT ANGLES IN A POLYGON

Doing hints   Get started. Draw some polygons. Be systematic. You will start to come up against unanswered questions such as: 'Convex or concave polygons?', 'All possible numbers of right angles or the maximum number?', 'Internal angles only?' The answers are up to you. Define the problem *you* want to tackle. Try to find a systematic way of producing successive polygons. Change your answers if you have a trivial problem. If you spot a pattern try to predict and prove. A word of warning – this investigation may lead you to a false conjecture, so a proof of your solution is essential! (Predict and check for polygons with 13, 14 and 15 sides.)

Class presentation hints
Age and ability: Third year upwards.
Materials: Lots of paper for drawing – plain, not squared; rulers; possibly a few protractors available to settle disputes!

Page 16 is relevant here. Finding their *own* way of systematically drawing the polygons is an important learning feature of this investigation. Don't tell them *your* way. Don't warn them of the false pattern either. If necessary suggest that they predict and verify the solutions for 13, 14, 15 sided polygons. The proof involves nothing more advanced than the sum of the interior angles of a polygon.

3 Taking an investigation into the classroom

Main aim

Your next step is now to choose one of the investigations you have worked with and plan how to present it to some pupils. The main, overriding aim for this particular lesson or sequence of lessons is for *you* to experience taking *your* investigation into *your* classroom. You can be confident that you are well prepared mathematically, although a pupil thinking from a different perspective may yet surprise you. None the less, give yourself the best chance of success: choose a class you enjoy teaching and with whom, under normal conditions, you rarely have management problems. Whatever class you choose, first-year to sixth form, the pupils will learn something from this new experience but, remember, *your* satisfaction is the focus of the task. No one but you can plan your lessons but, to aid you, the task of planning has been broken up into some of its component aspects and pertinent questions and statements are offered for your consideration.

Sub-aims

On this occasion:

1 What do you want your pupils to get out of this experience? 'Fun' is quite an acceptable answer but you might have other aims.
2 What do you want them to do?
3 What questions do you want them to answer?
4 What questions do you want them to ask?

Your answers to these questions might guide the way in which you structure your lessons.

Build-up

How do you want to introduce your pupils to investigations? Do you want to talk to your pupils about investigations in general and why you are getting them to do one? Alternatively, would you prefer to just go in with a specific investigation and get on with it? Teachers take different views about this.
  Before making this decision consider the following points:

● How are you intending to follow this investigation? Are you intending to use investigations on a regular basis? Or when they fit into the normal syllabus work? Or when the class needs a pick-me-up?

● Do you want the pupils to feel that investigations are a normal part of mathematics? Or that they are something special?

● Do you want to say anything about why investigations are important? If so, what?

How the class will work

Think carefully about the alternatives:

● If you do the investigation with the whole class you will be able to control to a certain extent the paths that the pupils follow and guide their discoveries, thus perhaps ensuring that everyone is gaining equally from the experience. You will also be presenting a gentle introduction to a new way of working, in an environment which does not challenge your powers of class management more actively than usual. There is, however, a danger that *you* will be doing it while the pupils just watch – and that is not a good way of getting them to think mathematically. Private working-time is important.

- If you expect the pupils to work individually, you will be offering them the chance to unravel and explore some mathematics for themselves. The surprises and successes will be their own but if they are unused to working in this way they will probably feel insecure and you will be rushed off your feet trying to get round to answer all the trivial and serious questions they will want to ask.

- If you get the pupils to work in groups, there will be the opportunity for them to work together, discuss strategies and pool ideas, but the class may get noisy and if they are not used to this way of working they may also not do very well. Collaboration and verbal communication are unfortunately not often features of the mathematics classroom.

- What about some combination of these methods of working? One structure for such a lesson is given in Chapter 1 (page 7).

Whichever method you choose, the lesson will need to be planned carefully.

Presenting the problem

Four presentations were illustrated in Chapter 2. The one used for your problem may well not be ideal for a class with little or no previous experience of doing investigations. To expect such pupils to work individually from a bald problem-statement is unrealistic.

You might, however, try a bald statement followed by a class discussion. Do not interpret the problem for them – the point of the class discussion will be for them to clarify the problem themselves.

If you offer a specific question to be answered, there is a danger that the investigation degenerates into a 'problem with a right answer', although this is unlikely with the investigations used so far. If this does happen your pupils will not be exploring what the problem is about.

If you dictate a series of suggestions to follow, there is a very real prospect of taking away opportunities for mathematical thinking, which provide much of the point of investigations. If you wish to use this kind of structure, make sure that the suggestions are provocative rather than prescriptive.

Getting the class started

Presenting the problem is only half the battle. If the pupils are new to this game, they need to know how to start. Their previous experience in mathematics classrooms may have been that tasks are clearly defined by instructions such as 'Draw a diagram', 'Plot a graph', 'Do exercise 17'. You will need, on this occasion, to offer them a specific starting strategy. Later, when they are more confident in this style of learning, they will be happy to select their own strategies.

Basically there are two possibilities:

1 You can offer a particular activity as in Presentation Method I (page 9). A more structured version of the polygons problem might be 'How many right angles can a shape with six sides have? What is the maximum number? What about seven-sided shapes? Eight-sided? etc.'

This approach allows individuals to work from a work sheet – a method of working with which they are, perhaps, at ease.

2 You can offer some examples to work from as in Presentation Method III. This can readily be done by exposition 'from the front' – a style of teaching with which both you and the class are probably familiar.

Whichever route you choose, everyone will be able to at least make a start.

Class-management

Pause a moment and consider:

- What behaviour do you expect from the pupils? Do you think they will want to talk to each other, or prefer to work alone?
- Might it be a good idea to warn your neighbours that there may be a higher noise-level than usual?
- What will you do about materials such as squared paper or calculators? Will you hand them out or wait for the pupils to ask for them?
- Think how the class might react to this new experience. Will they find it fun, or complain that it is not 'proper maths'? This latter is a very common reaction, so do not be alarmed – after all it *is* proper maths and not just 'school' maths!
- How are you going to cope with those who finish? This is where the need for extensions comes in and Appendix 2 offers some suggestions.
- How are you going to cope with those who get stuck? There is a great art in judging just how much help to give.

Answer a question with a question

A good way to encourage pupils to do their own thinking, rather than to rely on you for suggestions, is to answer their questions with questions. For instance:

- What do *you* think?
- What have you done so far?
- How did you get that?
- What have you tried?
- What other numbers (shapes, etc.) could you try?
- Can you explain that to me?
- Is there any other approach you could try?
- Have you looked for a pattern?
- Can you convince another pupil you are right?

As a last resort, offer not a single suggestion but a selection of possible moves from which the pupil can choose.

How long to spend

Do not over-estimate what the pupils will get done in a lesson! On the other hand they may surprise you with the amount of concentrated work they do. A good aim is that pupils should find some patterns fairly quickly. If there is a succession of personal discoveries, most pupils will be happy to keep going over a number of lessons. If they do not find anything they may get discouraged, although just what counts as a discovery is another matter – it may be something quite simple which pleases a pupil. In the 'Bogus billiards' problem (Chapter 1), for instance, low-ability pupils get a great deal of satisfaction from the different visual patterns produced by drawing the paths of the ball on tables of different sizes.

**Activity 3.1
Do it now!**

If you have not been doing it as you read through this chapter, plan your investigation lesson now.

Reflection

When you have taught the lesson, make notes about things that went well and things that did not go so smoothly. Here are some suggested headings for your notes:

- With whom it was done.
- How it was introduced.
- How long it took.
- How far the pupils got.
- How the pupils worked: alone, in groups, or as a whole class.
- Pupils' reactions to this mode of working.
- Your own feeling of success or failure.
- Organisational problems.
- Mathematical problems.
- Common questions – possible answers.
- Other teaching problems.
- Surprises, pleasant or unpleasant.

Finally, do be encouraged to try the lesson out, making any variations you think fit, with other classes.

Recording and writing-up

These two different activities are discussed in detail in Chapter 8. At this stage it is probably best, and definitely easiest, to allow the pupils to work in any way which they find suitable. Do not interfere with any *ad hoc* recording which they devise for themselves, although you may want to offer a couple of suitable systems to the anxious. A neat write-up is almost certainly not appropriate on this occasion.

4 Investigations dissected

This chapter considers the structure and stages of working within an investigation and seeks to illustrate the mathematical processes, that is to say, ways of thinking which are independent of syllabus or content, which are developed by mathematical investigations. It is a long and 'heavy' chapter and you are advised to read it through fairly superficially at first to form an impression of the structure before working more slowly through the text to gain greater understanding and insight.

The work involved in any piece of mathematical exploration or investigation can be broken down into four basic stages:

1 Understanding the problem
2 Getting started
3 Becoming involved
4 Reflecting and extending

It must be made very clear that the aim of this chapter is *not* to offer a prescription for 'teaching pupils how to do investigations'. No doubt it would be possible to analyse the structure exposed here and devise a sequence of rules and instructions which, if followed, would lead to an 'answer'. To do this would totally negate the intentions and enjoyment of mathematical investigations. Obtaining answers is not the aim of this way of working. As has already been stated it is the journey, with its deviations, diversions and discoveries, encouraging and enabling pupils to think mathematically, which is important. If you tell them how to get the answer, why not just tell them the answer?

The purpose of the analysis which follows is to open your eyes to some of the richness of mathematics lying within any good investigational problem and to offer you some methods of enabling pupils to work in new ways. For many of them, and possibly for you also, mathematics so far has been concerned with remembering and applying content and techniques, not with thinking and inventing.

Stage 1: Understanding the problem

Initially it will be your responsibility to ensure that pupils do understand the problem that is being presented to them for consideration. As they become used to working in exploratory and investigative ways, more able pupils will be capable of interpreting problems for themselves. Two strategies are recommended here. The first is to check that the vocabulary used in the problem statement is familiar to everyone. The 'Consecutive sums' problem in Chapter 2 was completely altered for one pupil who included $1 + 3 + 5 + 7 = 16$ and $2 + 4 + 6 = 12$ within her exploration, arguing that they were sums of consecutive numbers, albeit consecutive odd numbers in the first example and consecutive even numbers in the second. In this case, far from disaster ensuing, the misunderstanding led to further fascinating explorations – consecutive square numbers? consecutive prime numbers? Another pupil, however, not realising that a polygon was a closed figure, reduced the 'Right angles in a polygon' problem to a triviality. The second strategy suggested is to encourage the pupils to focus carefully on what information is or is not given in the problem statement. The polygon problem makes no mention of 'convex' or 'concave' shapes, nor of 'internal' or 'external' angles. Pupils may have to make assumptions of their own, but they must do this consciously.

Stage 2: Getting started

This is often the hardest stage for many! A clean sheet of paper can be very daunting. Once a start has been made, then the investigator is often carried along by the problem – but *how* to start? A foolproof, almost mechanical, method is offered, and you may decide initially to make the choices for your pupils. The secret is to have something specific to *do*.

EITHER:

(a) Turn the problem into a diagram,

e.g. in 'Dots and areas':

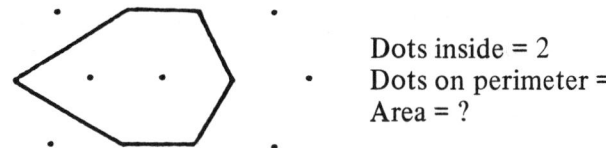

Dots inside = 2
Dots on perimeter = 6
Area = ?

This immediately indicates that the first step must be to devise a way of measuring the area. (This way of starting was used in 'Bogus billiards'.)

OR

(b) Put the problem in terms of an example,

e.g. in 'Consecutive sums':

$$5 = 2 + 3$$
$$9 = 2 + 3 + 4$$

Something is written down. It is easy now to carry on finding further sums, albeit possibly unsystematically to start with.

OR

(c) Turn 'Investigate' into a specific question and write it down,

e.g. in 'Consecutive sums': 'What numbers are they?'

This suggests a starting strategy of going through the numbers: '1? No', '2? No', '3? Yes, 3 = 1 + 2', etc.

OR

(d) Rewrite the problem in your own words,

e.g. in 'S-factors':

$$16 = 12 + 4 \qquad \text{and } 12 \times 4 = 48$$
$$16 = 5 + 7 + 3 + 1 \text{ and } 5 \times 7 \times 3 \times 1 = 105$$

Can I find S-factors of 16 which give a bigger number than 105?

OR

(e) Model the problem in some way with concrete materials. This method of starting will be used later in this chapter for a problem called 'Borders'.

When embarking on any ill-defined job it is always worth having to hand a varied collection of tools so that, as the need arises, an appropriate tool can be selected for use. Pupils need to build up through experimentation and experience such a collection of starting strategies: ways which they find useful for getting going on a problem. You can help them to do this by presenting them with a variety of problems which benefit from different approaches. Throughout this guide the recommended investigations have been carefully selected to highlight different aspects of the investigative processes, but below is a list of strategies for possible inclusion in your tool box. It is by no means exclusive – you will certainly want to add to it as you become more involved with investigations – but it will help you to be aware of the variety of ways of starting which are available to you.

Trial and error
Systematic organisation
Simplification
Representation: diagrams, tables, lists, drawings, etc.
Dividing the problem into separate chunks
Experimenting
Manipulating materials

Working backwards
Simulation, modelling
Transferring to a similar problem
Calculating, computing
Creating equations (a starting strategy only at sixth-form level and above)

The nature of a good investigation is to exploit and expose mathematical thinking. The term *processes* is used to cover these ways of thinking and it is the processes which you want to tease out and encourage in your pupils as they work on an investigation. There is no agreed list of processes among mathematicians but the more common terms are presented below.

A powerful way of entering into a problem and exposing its nature is to *specialise*: that is to say, select some simplified example of the problem and work on it in order to give a window on to the original task. In the problem 'S-factors', specialising would involve abandoning 16 to start with and working with 2, 3 and 4 to seek direction on how to approach the dissection of 16. *Organising* a systematic approach and appropriate representations for data can do much towards making it easier to *spot patterns* and relationships in your results. Systematically listing the results in the problem 'Consecutive sums' as follows: $1 + 2 = 3$, $2 + 3 = 5$, $3 + 4 = 7$ rapidly indicates a pattern. The next step is to *predict* further likely outcomes or *conjecture* reasons for the emerging laws. Thus an initial conjecture might be 'sums of two consecutive numbers are always odd'. Pupils are apt to overlook the need to *check, verify* and *prove* the validity of their conjectures. Whilst encouraging these activities, it must be made clear to the pupils that any conjecture is a good conjecture even if it subsequently proves to be incorrect. It is the process of making conjectures which is important. A sophisticated stage beyond that of predicting particular results is the ability to *generalise* from these results. One such generalisation in the problem 'Consecutive sums' would be 'the sum of any two consecutive numbers is always 1 plus twice the first number'. Further processes include *recording*, and *writing-up*, which are discussed in detail in Chapter 8, and *seeing, saying* and *reflecting*, all of which are discussed later in this chapter.

(Processes are in italics the first time they are mentioned in this chapter.)

Stage 3: Becoming involved

To enter the stage of 'Involvement' you need first to select your initial strategy and *strategy selection* is seen by many as a fundamental process in problem-solving. This stage is the main body of the structure and can itself be sub-divided into four phases:

1. Playing
2. Confirming
3. Seeing
4. Communicating

Each phase is built from a complicated interaction of different mathematical processes. It is unlikely that any investigation will naturally encompass all the processes to be described, but nonetheless I will use a single, particular, fairly simple investigation now as the clearest means of demonstrating the way through the phases of 'involvement'. The treatment which follows may at times seem a little forced and laborious, but the benefits of a single illustrative example outweigh this disadvantage. Try to work through the problem in parallel with the text, rather than jumping to a solution. The aim is to expose the thinking behind the acquisition of a solution.

Problem 4.1
Borders

How many 1 x 1 paving slabs would you need to make a border round a rectangular pond? (You may find cubes, square tiles and squared paper helpful.)

Stage 1 I have no problems here with the vocabulary (though some pupils may exclude squares from their definitions of rectangular). Notice that the problem does not say how wide the border should be. I will assume for now that it is one slab wide.

Stage 2 One way of starting might be to model the problem by drawing a rectangle and placing cubes or square tiles around to form the border. Here I will have to be content with a diagram.

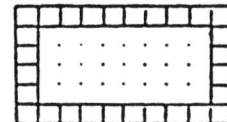

I now have to select a strategy to help me get started. 'Trial and error' is often the most useful starting tool to give one some feel for the problem, remembering that errors are not to be discouraged but, on the contrary, can be a valuable indication of the way forward.

Stage 3

PHASE 1: PLAYING

Playing should be a totally informal, unstructured activity – not usually encouraged in the mathematics classroom! For this reason you may find you need to prompt pupils with comments such as 'Just try it out', 'Do it and see what happens', 'Pick any number to start with'. This phase is often characterised by working in an oft-repeated loop:

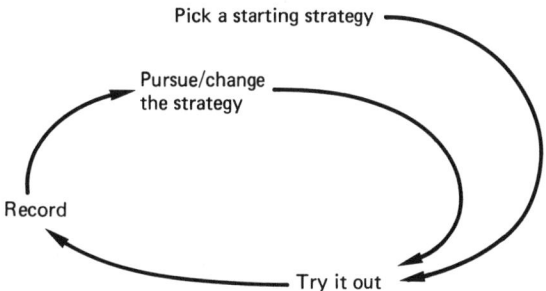

Remember that *recording* in this context means any appropriate method of reminding yourself what was happening as you played. In this phase any ideas are good ideas. Guess at fruitful approaches. Try out a variety of strategies. Flights of fancy and imagination are to be encouraged. A word of warning is needed, however – do not plunge into algebra too fast. Pupils are unlikely to do this, but older mathematicians can leap over the play phase and in so doing lose solutions and anomalies.

**Activity 4.1
Do it now!**

Play with the problem for 5 minutes. Actually draw some ponds. See how many slabs you need to make the borders.

**Activity 4.2
Do it now!**

Now look back at what you have been doing. Each time you drew a particular pond you were specialising.

- Did you in fact work round the loop?

- What and how did you record?
- Did you pursue the strategy of random trial, or did you perhaps change to some more systematic organisation?
- Did you simplify your approach?
- Did you change your strategy from using concrete materials to representation by drawing?

At this point *my* total record looks like this:

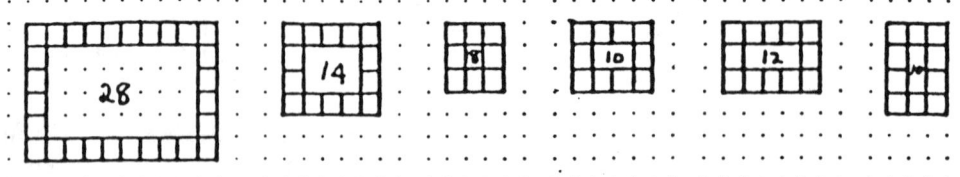

I have moved from random to simple and systematic drawing and am just entering the 'seeing' phase.

PHASE 2: SEEING

This phase begins when playing has led to a hunch as to 'how it might go' or to a definite idea for a strategy which might allow some pattern to be spotted. Usually the first thing that is needed is some *organisation* of the recording which exploits the organisation of the playing strategies. Displaying results in an ordered form definitely aids *pattern-spotting*.

Mathematics is essentially a study of patterns and laws – a view not often presented to pupils. Investigations encourage the seeking of such relationships. A carefully chosen investigation can also give rise to all kinds of work on representation. The values to be examined are from pupils' own choices of specialisation, and data presentation is motivated by the desire to spot their own patterns and trends in the mathematics they are creating. Pupils who can go no further than this can still be proud of their own mathematics. Such pupils are also in a position to follow further developments by their peers, even if they themselves could not carry out the more advanced stages of the investigation. This is one of the major strengths of investigations: they offer success at many levels and this is invaluable, particularly in mixed-ability groups.

Activity 4.3
Do it now!

Go back to your recordings so far and decide whether some other form of representation would enable you to spot any patterns or relationships which might exist between the dimensions of the ponds and the number of slabs on their borders.

By now you may have 'seen' the relationship between side-length and number of slabs. What follows will therefore seem somewhat contrived. The intention is to illustrate the use of different mathematical thinking processes, *not* to suggest that this is the most appropriate method of teaching this particular problem.

I have opted for a matrix based on the pond's dimensions, with the cells containing the number of slabs needed.

So far my table is rather sparsely and randomly filled. Nonetheless I can make a couple of *conjectures* about patterns which I can see emerging. The first arises directly from my diagrams: 'the number of slabs needed is inde-

22

	1	2	3	4	5	6	7	8
1	8	10	12					
2	10		14					
3								
4								28
5								

Horizontal

Vertical

pendent of the orientation of the pond'. This hunch is based on one pair of examples, the 2 x 1 and 1 x 2 ponds.

The second conjecture is based on a slight pattern I can see developing in the first row of my matrix. I predict that the entry for 1 x 4 pond will be 14, 1 x 5 pond will be 16, etc. At this point I should be moving into the 'confirming' phase.

PHASE 3: CONFIRMING

Conjectures can be wild guesses, flashes of insight or deductions based on very little evidence. All of these are permissible, even to be encouraged, as long as they are always followed up by *checking* through further specialisation, or *verification* by reasoned argument.

These processes of conjecturing and checking may need to be repeated many times but pupils are frequently reluctant to become involved in a procedure which has a high error rate. They do not want to be 'wrong'. It is their experience that, if they wait, the teacher will tell them the right way so they have concluded that mathematics is about 'getting the right answer'. At first therefore your pupils will need constant reassurance that it is 'having the hunch' which indicates success, followed by checking its validity. The fact that it did not completely fit the situation is far less important.

**Activity 4.4
Do it now!**

Go back to your results at the 'seeing' stage and try to make some conjecture or prediction from emerging patterns. Check your conjectures by specialising or explaining. Can you see a rule emerging for calculating the number of slabs needed for any pond? Look either at your number patterns, or at the way you are drawing your ponds. Try to write the rule down in words first, then try to write it algebraically.

I, too, ought to go back and check my conjectures with some more examples. The question for discussion is 'How many examples do I need to verify my conjecture?' A general answer might be 'As many as it takes for you to be confident or able to see why the conjecture must hold.' An anecdote illustrates the dilemma:
Conjecture: All odd numbers are prime.
Verification: 1 is prime, 3 is prime, 5 is prime, 7 is prime, 9 is . . . not prime, but one must allow for experimental error, 11 is prime, 13 is prime. I am convinced!

In this investigation I am totally confident that lengths are unaltered by movement in the plane and so the orientation of the pond is quite irrelevant. Working from this conjecture I can actually fill in some more cells in my matrix, which will be symmetrical about the diagonal.

For my second conjecture I will draw the 1 x 4 and 1 x 5 ponds.

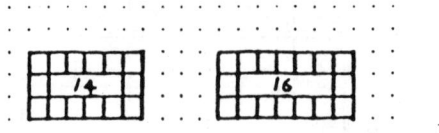

Hurrah!

I am now convinced that the number of tiles goes up by 2 as the side length goes up by 1. I have in fact just *generalised* my conjecture from a few examples to a rule for predicting the number of squares round any pond. I could write the rule in an alternative fashion thus:

The number of tiles needed round a pond is 2 more than the number round a pond 1 unit shorter.

This in fact helps me to a more useful generalisation: one from which I can predict the number of slabs for any pond:

Number of tiles round pond length n =
number of tiles round pond length 1, plus $2 \times (n - 1)$ =
$8 + 2(n - 1)$.

If you laid your paving slabs down in a different system from mine then your conjectured rule may well be different. Does it result in the same numerical answers?

PHASE 4: COMMUNICATING

This phase does not follow on from phase 3 but should in fact be taking place during all or any of phases 1, 2 or 3. Communication can take place in one of several ways at different levels and stages. Many, probably, most, people find it hard to express mathematical ideas in language, so that before beginning to write about mathematics the transition from 'seeing' to *saying* can be a major hurdle. It is at this stage that pupil–pupil discussion, dialogue in language at the level of pupils' thinking, can be of great value. Pupils can provide each other with a less threatening audience than the teacher, yet still be a source of questions, demands for clarification, and suggestions of counter-examples. In trying to say what they are doing, pupils develop ideas, or errors become apparent. It is the lack of opportunity to talk about their mathematics which inhibits many pupils from attempting to write about their findings.

The saying or *writing* can span the spectrum from a brief account of what was done to a rigorous proof of results and testing of hypotheses. All forms are valuable. Somewhere towards the latter end comes communication through symbolisation, the method generally seen as the only means of communicating mathematics. This should not be offered to pupils until they see a need for some form of shorthand. Writing down in their own words and later their own symbols is far more valuable in allowing pupils to create and understand their personal mathematics. Methods of communication via graphs, tables, models, too, need to be encouraged. Even a simple diagram, such as this

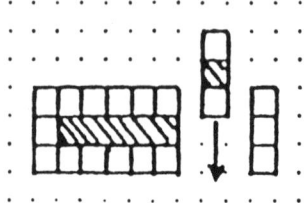

for the borders rule discussed above, can encapsulate an explanation or conjecture.

Scant mention has been made of the place of proof. It is the response to the question 'How do you know you are right?' *Verification* and *justification* should be encouraged but at a level appropriate to the particular pupil with a particular piece of mathematics. The relevant level of proving might be indicated by one of the following questions:

(i)   can you convince a friend?
(ii) can you convince an enemy?
(iii) can you convince a mathematician?

Stage 4: Reflecting and extending

For most pupils mathematical activities tend to stop at the end of stage 3. The teacher will pass judgement and suggest the next activity. Reflection is one of the key features of this guide and ideally it should also be an automatic consequence of 'doing' some mathematics for all pupils. Some of the features of reflection are encouraged by a need to communicate. Some appropriately probing remarks are:

- 'Tell a friend what you did.'
- 'Explain what steps you took.'
- 'Can you remember what you were thinking at that point?'
- 'Have you left anything out?'
- 'Are there any questions you want to ask that you have not yet found an answer for?'

If you wish your pupils to produce a formal write-up of their work then this is probably the moment to suggest it.

PHASE 1: REFLECTING

Looking back over *my* write-up of 'Borders' I notice that my second conjecture was based on ponds of unit width only, and I have not, in fact, actually considered wider ponds at all when conjecturing; neither, however, have I made this explicit. Indeed, my generalisation is defined only in terms of length, which is not enough to specify a single rectangle. I need to go back to do some further specialising and fill up the table a little more in order to make a conjecture relating to all possible ponds.

This kind of omission is very common in any investigational work. You will find that as you make choices and specialise in certain directions you inevitably leave loose ends behind and there is nothing wrong in this as long as you are aware or intend to look over your work at some later stage.

Activity 4.5
Do it now!

Look back over your 'Borders' investigation. Have you, like me, left any loose ends?

PHASE 2: EXTENDING

In any teaching situation you are likely to have a pupil with the question, 'I have finished that, what can I do now?'. With any good investigation you will always have an answer to this question! Obviously, the answer will often be of the form 'Are you sure?' 'Can you write down why?', 'Have you reflected on your work?', but for the more able pupil you can be confident that you have a genuine extension of the investigation up your sleeve.

The initial approach should be to check whether any particular assumptions were made at the start of the investigation. In this case I assumed the border to be 1 slab wide. I could therefore now investigate the problem of laying borders of different widths.

In general, a very powerful method of creating extensions to a problem is to ask the question 'What if not?'. Take the problem statement. Go through it word by word asking the question 'What if not "word"?' and replace that word by some other appropriate word.

To illustrate this technique using the problem 'Borders', do as follows:

'How many 1 × 1 . . .?' STOP. What-if-not 1 × 1? TRY 'How many 1 × 2 slabs . . .?'

Carry on:

'How many 1 × 2 slabs would you need to make a border round a rectangular . . .?' STOP. What-if-not rectangular? TRY 'L-shaped' pond.

'How many 1 × 2 slabs would you need to make a border round an L-shaped pond?' – a new investigation.

In fact in a more general form:

'How many $n \times m$ slabs are needed for border t slabs wide round a "specified" shaped pond?'

When seeking an extension to explore, it is not, of course, necessary to completely transform the problem by doing 'what-if-not' to more than one word at a time. In this case you could try 1 × 2 slabs round a rectangular pond *or* 1 × 1 slabs round an L-shaped pond.

An afterthought: what-if-not a two-dimensional pond?

In the words of the physicist P. Anderson:

I have yet to see a problem, however complicated, which, when you looked at it in the right way, did not become still more complicated!

Activity 4.6
Do it now!

Try any extension of 'Borders' that interests you.

Summary

The basic stages of an investigation:

1 Understanding the problem:
   (a) Check the vocabulary.
   (b) Focus on what information is or is not given.

2 Getting started:
   (a) Turn the problem into a diagram.
   (b) Put the problem in terms of an example.
   (c) Turn "investigate" into a question.
   (d) Rewrite the question in your own words.
   (e) Model the problem with concrete materials.

Look in your tool box (pages 19–20) for useful strategies.

3 Becoming involved:
   (a) Playing.
   (b) Seeing.
   (c) Confirming.
   (d) Communicating.

4 Reflecting and extending:
   (a) Look back for omissions and assumptions.
   (b) What-if-not?

The processes
   Selecting starting strategies
   Specialising
   Organising

Pattern-spotting
Predicting and conjecturing
Checking and verifying
Proving
Recording
Writing-up
Seeing
Saying
Reflecting
Generalising
Extending

5 Investigations which focus on a particular process

Use the vocabulary of processes

In case you are in any doubt, it is definitely not suggested that you should ever drive pupils through an investigation in the manner used in the previous chapter! Neither is it a good idea to introduce them to the stages and processes in this way. However, if you want pupils to be able to reflect on their investigational work, if you want them to be able to talk about what they have done, if you want them to ask questions about 'how?' and 'why?', and not just 'what?' then you must give them the vocabulary to use. Positive attitudes can be built up by making explicit processes which are shown to be of value in the study of mathematics. 'Guess' carries an aura of 'not knowing', of 'hoping to avoid failure', of mathematics being a 'hit and miss affair', but talk about 'conjectures', 'predictions', 'hypotheses' and you have instant academic respectability. The public image of mathematics is of precision, not 'trial and error', but talk of 'specialising' and you have a legitimate technique. Do not underestimate either the power of the public image to form pupils' attitudes or the power of words to direct their thinking and reform their personal images within the given social climate. A true anecdote may help to emphasise this point. A class of second year pupils, having worked all year with a teacher who uses exclusively an investigative teaching style, were within a couple of weeks of their end-of-year exams. The teacher was confronted by a boy saying 'Everyone else is doing revision. Can we do some too?' She replied 'Fine. What would you like to revise?' Back came the reply 'Well, give us a completely new investigation and then we can revise conjecturing.'

Use the vocabulary of investigations freely in your own speech. There is no need to present it formally unless you wish. When you hear pupils using the terminology with each other, then you will know that you have won.

'Practise' processes

Pupils who are accustomed to didactic, directive teaching are bound to feel insecure at first in an unstructured situation. In Chapter 3 ways were suggested of structuring the 'starting' stage of the particular investigation you were planning. Your aim should be to gradually wean the pupils away from your support, but this can only be achieved if that support is replaced by a structure which they can build for themselves. You may find it helpful to focus from time to time on one specific process, thus allowing pupils to concentrate on and internalise some of the aspects of mathematics which are not content-related. The remainder of this chapter looks at investigations which enable you to do this.

Activity 5.1
Do it now!

Consider the following sequence of matchstick models:

**Problem 5.1
Sequences**

Make or draw the next two models in the sequence. Can you predict what the 8th model will look like?
Check your conjecture.
Predict and check the 11th and 16th models.

What about the 32nd model? Can you predict how many matches you will need without making all the preceding models?
Can you justify your conjecture?
Can you generalise your results?

Conjecture, check, generalise

The mini-investigation you have just done can be used to focus pupils' thinking either on the processes of conjecture and checking, or on generalising. Present pupils with lots of different sequences – some ideas are given below – and ask them to answer the questions you have just answered. If you wish to concentrate on conjecturing then omit the last two questions. This series of similar short investigations, although fairly structured in approach, will give pupils a quick insight into the satisfaction of spotting patterns in mathematics, and can be used with any age or ability since you can offer sequences of appropriate complexity to individual pupils.

Ideas: *Matchsticks*

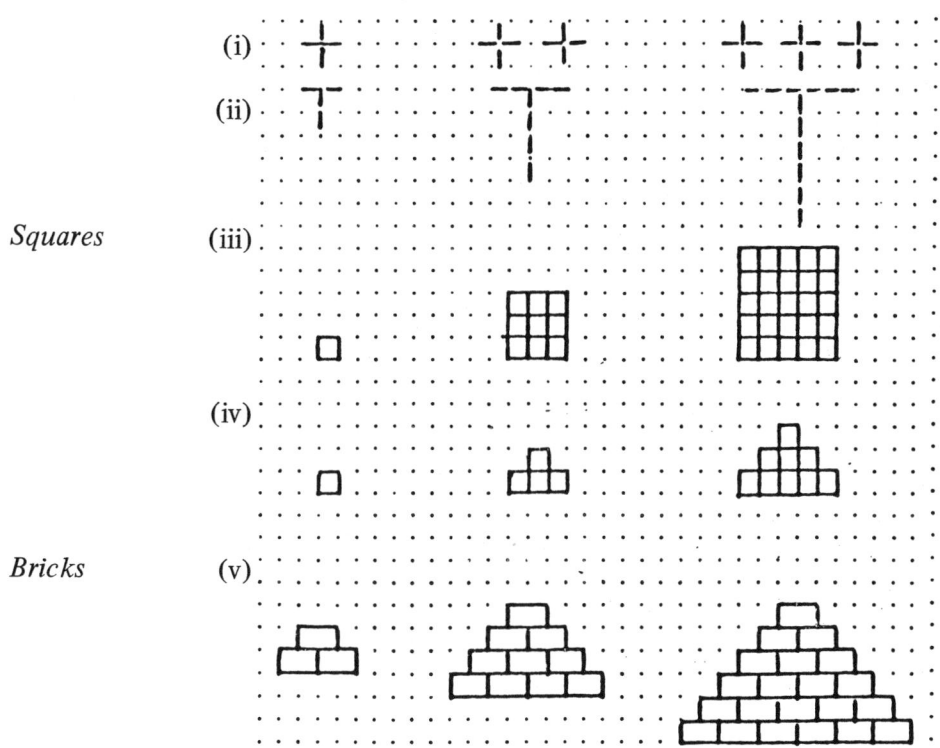

Squares (iii)

(iv)

Bricks (v)

Invent some more for yourself, the possibilities are endless!

Below are four investigations, each of which has been chosen to focus on a particular process.

**Problem 5.2
Choose a number**

(An investigation focusing on conjecturing.)
Choose any whole number. Add 8. Divide by 3. If you continue adding 8 and dividing by 3, what do you think will happen? Use a calculator to check

your conjecture. Choose another number. What will happen now if you repeatedly add 8 and divide by 3?

Carry on choosing and predicting.

Problem 5.3
Investigating the 100 square

(An investigation focusing on pattern-seeking and relationships.)

Draw a box round any 2 x 2 square of numbers as illustrated.

1	2	3	4	5	6	7	8	9	10
11	12	13	14	15	16	17	18	19	20
21	22		24	25	26	27	28	29	30
31	32	33	34	35	36	37	38	39	40
41	42	43	44	45	46	47	48	49	50
51	52	53	54	55	56	57	58	59	60
61	62	63	64	65	66	67	68	69	70
71	72	73	74	75	76	77	78	79	80
81	82	83	84	85	86	87	88	89	90
91	92	93	94	95	96	97	98	99	100

What relationships do you notice between the corner numbers? Draw another 2 x 2 box and look again for relationships between the corner numbers.

Specialise some more. Can you see any general pattern emerging?

What about 3 x 3 boxes? 4 x 4 boxes?

Problem 5.4
Painted cube

(An investigation focusing on generalising.)

The whole of the outside of a 3 by 3 by 3 cube is painted red. If the cube is cut up into unit cubes, how many of the unit cubes have:

4 faces red?
3 faces red?
2 faces red?
1 face red?
No red face?

Now consider a painted 2 x 2 x 2 cube.

How about a 4 x 4 x 4 cube?

Can you predict the number of unit cubes with 4, 3, 2, 1 and no red faces on a 7 x 7 x 7 cube?

Can you find a way of telling how many of each sort of unit cube there will be in *any* big cube?

Write down the rules in words.

Express the rules symbolically.

Problem 5.5
Chains

(An investigation focusing on specialising.)

For any integer n, $\quad n \rightarrow 3n + 1$ if n is odd
$\qquad\qquad\qquad n \rightarrow n/2 \quad$ if n is even.

Investigate.

Activity 5.2
Do it now!

Choose just one of these investigations. As in Chapter 2 the aim is for you to delve deeply into a single problem rather than get an overview of several. Spend at least three-quarters of an hour on this – more if you want. Write down all your conjectures, however tentative, and any patterns that you think are emerging. The investigations have all been given a certain amount of structure in order that you should focus on particular processes. On this occasion *only*, try not to be sidetracked by your own ideas. Nevertheless, enjoy yourself!

Before you move on to planning your investigation for a class, there are two more brief activities for you to do.

**Activity 5.3
Do it now!**

Turn back to Chapter 2, page 11 and, using the same questions as before, reflect on what you have just done.
Are your replies different from last time?

**Activity 5.4
Do it now!**

Go through the problem statements of 'Choose a number' and 'Painted cube' and do a 'what-if-not' to produce some extensions for these investigations.

Some notes are given on each of these investigations in the Appendix below. You may like to look at them before the next activity.

**Activity 5.5
Do it now!**

Plan the investigation you did for one of your classes. Remember the primary aim is for them to focus on a particular mathematical process, so structure your presentation and their way of working to achieve this.

Reflection

When you have given this investigation to a class, turn back to Chapter 3, page 17 and make some notes on how the lessons went. Use the headings given to help you. Were you successful in your primary aim?

Appendix to Chapter 5

SEQUENCES

Doing hints To spot a pattern in the way the sequences extend, watch *how* you draw the next model. This will give you a relationship relating the nth term u_n of the sequence to the previous one. Now try to reduce this to a relationship involving only the first term and the ordinal number of the term (i.e. u_n in terms of u_1 and n, not just u_{n-1}).

Class presentation hints
Age and ability: Anyone. Make the sequences as simple or as hard as you like. Just being able to continue the patterns will be a challenge for the less able.
Materials: Concrete materials such as matchsticks, cubes, blocks or coins.

This is an ideal investigation to present via a work sheet. Activity 5.1 on pages 28-9 suggests a possible wording. As an extension, challenge the pupils to devise sequences for each other.

CHOOSE A NUMBER

Doing hints This focuses on conjecture, so go ahead and guess and *write down* what you think will happen. It does not matter if you are wildly wrong! The aim is that, as you do this with other combinations of numbers, you will start to see a trend and so get better at guessing or predicting. Use a calculator rather than a micro to start with so that you can look at the effect of each repeated + 8 and ÷ 3. A word of warning if your calculator has

algebraic logic (i.e. if 2 + 3 × 4 = 14): you need the key sequence

$\boxed{+}$ $\boxed{8}$ $\boxed{=}$ $\boxed{-}$ $\boxed{3}$ with an optional extra $\boxed{=}$ after the $\boxed{3}$. When you

'see' what is happening, a five-line program for the micro will speed up the production of results, BUT do conjecture first for each new starting value or change of addendum or divisor. If you think in terms of fractions rather than decimals you may spot the patterns more quickly.

Class presentation hints
Age and ability: Anyone.
Materials: Lots of calculators; micro if possible.

A good investigation for introducing or practising with the calculator. The mathematical ideas of iteration and convergence are embedded in the exploration. Conversion of decimals to fractions is useful. After a class introduction to the problem you might suggest they all choose their own starting number and then do + 8 ÷ 3 and see what happens. After that, cooperative working, in groups or as a class, helps to fill in the table more quickly. Try to insist that they write down their guesses first and emphasise that it does not matter how wrong they are! An alternative start might be to try + 1 ÷ 2 as 'Chinese Whispers' round the class using fractions. Listen to their comments. Proof of the emerging 'rule' involves the sum to infinity of a geometric progression. For younger or less able pupils suggest that they focus on the divisors 2, 3, 4, 5 as the fraction conversions are more obvious for these numbers. If pupils want to try 'outrageous' sequences like + 99 ÷ 760 then don't discourage them. With a calculator they can choose *any* number and still see the convergence.

INVESTIGATING THE 100 SQUARE

Doing hints   Look for multiplicative, as well as additive, relationships. What about relationships between corner numbers and the centre number in any 3 × 3 square?

Class presentation hints
Age and ability: Anyone.
Materials: Lots of copies of the 100 square; blank squared paper.

An alternative to drawing a box on the 100 square is to cut a hole in a sheet of squared paper and place it over the 100 square, revealing the *n* × *n* square to be explored. No relationship is too trivial. The aim is to spot patterns and 'the top two corners are consecutive numbers' or 'the left-hand corners both end in the same number' are both patterns. Try to gently push the pupils on to say why they think this is the case. More complex relationships require algebra in their proof and if you insist on rigour this investigation can be a challenge at sixth form level. You may well be surprised by some of the patterns your pupils see. Do not discourage those who wander away from the *n* × *n* square and start looking at other patterns. The 100 square is amazingly rich in patterns!

PAINTED CUBE

Doing hints   Use centicubes or multifix cubes to help if you need them, or draw the cube on isometric paper. Devise a counting system. How can you check your results? A table helps with prediction and generalisation.

Class presentation hints

Age and ability: Anyone.

Materials: Lots of cubes are essential; isometric paper in case they ask for it. Plastic cubes have the advantage that they can be marked with pen or sticky paper and easily cleaned again.

The major hurdle for many pupils is how to count their unit cubes. Encourage them to invent a system. Also encourage them to devise a checking procedure and, if necessary, suggest tabulating the results. For the larger cubes counting the cubes with no red faces poses problems. One way to do this is to build the cube and actually 'peel off' the outside layer. You may be surprised how few pupils see the connection between a $3 \times 3 \times 3$ physical cube and the number 3^3, obtained by cubing 3. Keep a check on the language the pupils use: face, edge, corner, and especially 'side'. An alternative approach to this problem is to actually make a cube with a red outside surface, break it up, and allow the pupils to reassemble it.

CHAINS

Doing hints   A common way of starting this investigation is to work through the whole numbers systematically. A useful method of recording is to combine the chains of numbers into a 'tree' with 'branches'. This way you only have to write down each number once. When you have a feel for the investigation you might want to work backwards – in other words, starting at 1, work out where each number in the chain has come from. What happens at branch points? Organise your recording method so that you can compare easily numbers which take the same number of steps to reach a branch point. Is there any relationship between numbers and the length of chains they generate?

Class presentation hints

Age and ability: Anyone.

Materials: Large sheets of paper – lines or squares can help to keep the tree tidy. Calculators are desirable or the class may find the arithmetic tedious. A micro will speed things up considerably, but don't start with this.

One way of introducing the investigation is with a flow diagram, particularly if this device has not been met before or the rule can be introduced in words. In either case, make sure everyone knows what 'odd' and 'even' mean. Even using calculators, arithmetical errors may creep in. Encouraging pupils to compare chain lengths with each other can act as a check on accuracy. Devising a useful recording system is important, but let pupils do this for themselves. The dramatically varying lengths of the chains becomes evident early in the investigation and this may prompt some pupils to look for the longest chain. Can they be sure that all numbers will form a chain down to 1? Proof of this and of the relationships between lengths of chains generated, for instance, by consecutive numbers calls for sophisticated algebraic representation and argument.

6 Classroom management

Investigations: when and how

This chapter is concerned with the question of finding, or making, time for investigations to become part of your schemes of work for all secondary pupils. It also has some guidance on your role as a teacher whilst investigations are going on in your classroom.

It is frequently argued that investigations take too long and so take away the time needed to teach the syllabus. To help you consider this problem, here are six suggested ways of using investigations.

A *To study a topic through investigations*

Such an approach usually takes one to two weeks and you might well find this very hard to do initially. When helping pupils to develop new concepts or acquire new skills, it is not easy to replace *all* the exposition you naturally give by open investigation. However, some topics do lend themselves to this treatment, although you might wish to impose some structure on to the work they are doing.

An example: The study of 2-dimensional shapes: for first-year pupils. (Materials needed: 9-pin geoboards, rubber bands, dotty paper)
How many different three-sided, then four-sided shapes can be made on a geoboard? Record them on dotty paper.

This will lead to discussion of 'different' and intuitive use of transformations to check on 'sameness'. Ideas of similarity and enlargement will be exposed and the results can form a class display. The only exposition needed from the teacher will be to tell the class the names conventionally used to describe their shapes. Pupils will, moreover, be anxious to acquire this information to enable them to discuss their shapes with each other. The content objectives of recognising the properties of triangles and quadrilaterals and classifying and naming them will have been generally covered. The scheme *Journey into Maths* (Shell Centre for Mathematical Education, University of Nottingham) covers the whole of the first and second year mathematics using largely investigations or an investigational approach.

B *To introduce a topic through an investigation*

Such an investigation can set the scene for a piece of mathematics or create in the pupils a *need* to develop their mathematics in a particular way. They may develop a feeling for the concept and be ready, motivated and interested to learn more.

An example: The investigation on sequences of shapes given in Chapter 5 creates a real need for early algebra. Pupils reach a stage where they need a shorthand and try to develop one – and then are ready to hear what conventions 'real' mathematicians use.

C *To partially study a topic through investigation*

In this case, the regular teaching of a topic may be interrupted for a lesson or two while the pupils investigate one aspect of it.

An example: What shapes can you make with 20 triangles?
For pupils working on areas of triangles and parallelograms this creates an interesting interlude.

D *To follow up or extend a topic by an investigation*

Once a topic has been grasped, at least partially, then investigations can be used to consolidate or extend a pupil's understanding. This is particularly useful when some members of a group still require time to come to grips with a topic while the more able are ready to move forward.

An example: Areas and perimeters
'Numerically, the perimeter of a rectangle is less than the area.'
Is this true:
- (a) always – if so, why?
- (b) sometimes – if so, when?
- (c) never – if so, why not?

E *To practise and consolidate a skill or concept*

Many investigations require routine, repetitious use of specific mathematical skills. Often such investigations provide the motivation for pupils to do the required practice, frequently without realising this is what they are doing!

An example: Can you find a number with 13 factors?
Use this to replace 'Exercise 3b. Factorise the following numbers . . . .' In addition to practice in factorisation, the pupils will gain a better understanding of the nature of factors and the composition of numbers.

The foregoing five ways of using investigations are all related to the contents of the syllabus you have to teach, since this is the concern of this chapter, but it would leave you with a totally false impression of the place of investigations in your teaching if a sixth category were not also included.

F *To create enjoyment of mathematics*

Pupils need to see that mathematics is not merely about learning the syllabus but also involves developing strategies and logical thinking and above all occasionally having fun!

An example: Can you always win at noughts and crosses?
'Bogus billiards' also falls into this category.

How to incorporate investigations into your teaching

Having become aware of *when* it might be appropriate to introduce an investigation into your teaching, you now need to consider *how* to do this. Some fairly painless ways are suggested below.

(1) *One lesson a week*
In favour of this is its regularity – the pupils may well look forward to the break from 'real maths' and they would steadily acquire the skills needed for investigations. You would be offering them a varied, balanced diet of mathematics. On the other hand an insertion in the existing programme of work could be artificial and frustrating if an investigation could not be allowed to spill over into the next period. In addition, any chance of looking at extensions would be very limited.

(2) *Part or whole of one topic a term*
Regularity is again an argument in favour of this method, but now time can also be made available for extensions and the discontinuity between investigations and syllabus work is avoided. If you use this method, plan well in advance, since some topics lend themselves better to this treatment than others.

(3) *Fun between topics*

This is certainly better than nothing. There is an inherent danger, though, that investigations are then not seen by pupils as real mathematics but are reduced to the status of puzzles. Of course if you do not present them under this title to the class it is certainly possible for the pupils to integrate the approach into their picture of mathematics.

(4) *One week per term*

This has the advantages of pleasurable expectation (as in (1), above) and of extended time. You can use topic-related or strategy-based investigations as you wish. Consider the idea of all your classes doing the same investigation at the same time. Most good investigations are suitable for this treatment. In fact some mathematics departments organise an investigation week for the whole school with a circus of problems available to everyone.

When you are confident of handling an investigative teaching style, you should aim to include adventitious investigations in your repertoire. These are investigations that just happen. Perhaps the ideal is one arising out of a pupil's question, 'What happens if . . .?' In this case it is totally relevant to the class, and probably to the topic you are covering too. There will also be times when you yourself become enthusiastic about an investigation, which has come from reading, from another teacher or has been brought to you by a pupil. Your own enthusiasm could be infectious, especially if it was pupil-initiated.

However and whenever you choose to use investigations in your teaching, remember that they can be made suitable for *all* pupils, the more and the less able, whether they be grouped by mixed ability, setted or banded.

The teacher's role

What part do you play in all of this? As always, you have many roles to play in the classroom, although, when working with investigations, they may differ from those 'normally' expected of you.

(1) *The role of instigator*
Give time and thought to your preparation.

The introduction must be good so that the pupils become quickly involved. You need to be clear about your objectives in terms of the mathematics they might use, the strategies they might adopt and the processes on which they might focus. Check that you have the necessary resources available, for example calculators, dotty paper, cubes.

Plan how you intend to end the lesson, even if it is only 'Carry on till the bell and we will discuss it next time', but be flexible and able to respond to any surprise that occurs. Have extensions or alternatives ready for the faster or brighter pupils.

(2) *The role of enabler*
Change the image both you and the class may have of your classroom authority.

You should be an 'enabler' not a 'provider'. Your aim is to have them thinking mathematically, not to fill them with the mathematical thoughts of others. You are, however, responsible for the investigation being accessible to all the pupils. Having ensured this, to the best of your ability, you also need to see that the resources and the lay-out of the room suit the work. You should be aware of the skills and techniques which will normally be needed in an investigation and those specifically appropriate to the investigation in hand. Later (much later) you will need to help them towards conventional terms and notation.

(3) *The role of facilitator*
Create the right atmosphere. The pupils need:

- freedom to be 'wrong' – there is no shame attached to a wrong conjecture;

- time to think at their own pace and level – this is rarely available in a traditional lesson;

- opportunity to discuss freely with peers and teachers – try suggesting that problems be discussed with other pupils before turning to you;

- the realisation that it is ideas and not answers that should be shared – a good slogan is: *Don't spoil other people's fun!*

(4) *The role of listener*

It is most important that you really listen to pupils. Really listen, do not just *hear* what you expect. Follow their reasoning if you can.

The aim is for *you* to get involved in *their* thoughts, not the other way round. If you cannot follow the explanation you are being given, do not jump in with your reinterpretation. See if any other pupils can help you to understand. Avoid interrupting, and do not prevent them from going down blind alleys – these can be important learning situations. The less overtly passive side of your role is to be ready to step in and re-motivate pupils if their results are disappointing. To be effective here, you need to be aware, if you can, of where in the processes their difficulties lie.

(5) *The role of questioner*

Your role is to ask pupils questions which help them to think but which avoid giving them the answer, for example:

- What do you think?
- What would you like the question to mean?
- How did you get there?
- What have you tried?
- What rule do you want to use?
- Have you thought about . . .?
- Do you remember anything we did last time?

If possible, answer a question with a question. See also Chapter 3 (page 14).

(6) *The role of positive evaluator*

Give the pupils the feeling of *success*. Probably your major role in terms of authority is to be responsible for pupils realising what they have learned.

This may be extremely hard. You yourself may not be sure what learning has taken place. In a traditional lesson the content is usually quite explicit, multiplying decimals or Pythagoras' theorem, say, and you are in a position to pass judgements on who has learned what. Success can be correlated with right answers. With investigations, pupils must be given the feeling of success at whatever level they are working. To spot a pattern, to make a conjecture whether it checks or not, to explain an idea to a friend, are all achievements and pupils need to realise this if they are not to be focused only on getting a right answer.

Do not base your judgement on their written work alone; watch and listen, too. To encourage pupils to value their own ideas you may need to act *positively* saying, for instance, 'I am sure you are telling me something which is going to help,' or 'Show me what you are trying to do.'

(7) *The role of observer*

Consciously develop your skills of observation. Do not judge, but use the opportunity provided by investigations to get to know your pupils better. Eavesdrop unobtrusively on the discussion between pupils. Ask yourself:

- Can they cooperate?
- Can they lead?

- Does one person do all the talking?
- Who makes all the suggestions?
- Do they spend time thinking?
- Do they listen to each other?
- Who makes decisions in a group?
- How do they make decisions?
- Can they defend their ideas?
- Can they counter others' ideas?
- How well do they settle?

By quiet listening you may spot an appropriate moment to introduce mathematical language, but do not interfere at any point which might interrupt the flow of mathematical thinking.

Although one of your aims is to enable pupils to evaluate themselves and their own work, you will undoubtedly at some point be cast in the role of assessor. This is most certainly not your role at present, and so this topic is postponed until Chapter 10, when it is covered in detail.

Appendix to Chapter 6

EXAMPLE C: SHAPES WITH 20 TRIANGLES

Doing hints   As with the polygon on page 9, you need to define your own problem before you can start. Single shapes which use all 20 triangles? Shapes each using up to 20 triangles? Shapes with the same area? What shapes can be made simultaneously using exactly 20 triangles? The first is probably the hardest problem, the last the easiest. What will the 20 triangles be? equilateral? isosceles? right-angled? congruent? similar? When are the shapes you make 'different'?

Class presentation hints
Age and ability: First or second years.
Materials: Scissors; printed sheets of triangles; isometric paper; compasses; rulers; protractors. Possibly plain paper and glue.

If you do not provide isometric paper, then one of your objectives could be to practise ruler and compass constructions. Allow plenty of time for this. Leave the pupils to decide for themselves what interpretation they place on the problem and pull out ideas of equal area, congruence, and similarity from whatever they produce. A wall display makes a good end point to this investigation. An alternative approach could be to try to cover various shapes with identical but possibly scalene triangles as a means of measuring areas.

EXAMPLE D: AREAS AND PERIMETERS

Doing hints   Play with sides with actual numbers as measurements to get an idea of whether the answer is (a), (b) or (c). Algebra can help to illuminate this problem. Are the area and perimeter ever numerically equal? You might find plotting a graph useful. What about circles? triangles?

Class presentation hints
Age and ability: First and second years at a numerical level, up to sixth form for an analytic solution.
Materials: None.

As an extension or follow-up investigation for first or second years working with area and perimeter this works best in pairs – be prepared for some heated arguments! Lots of specialising is needed to 'see' what is happening. What if the lengths of the sides of the rectangles are not whole numbers? One idea for recording might be to plot one side against the other using different colours according to whether the pairs give area greater than, equal to, or less than perimeter. At a higher level, there is interesting work involving conditions for inequalities, boundary values and a graph worth plotting.

EXAMPLE E: 13 FACTORS

Doing hints   Specialise! Factorise simple numbers. Clearly, if you reduce the problem to 13 prime factors it becomes trivial. Beware of algebra too early. What numbers of factors *can* you have?

Class presentation hints
Age and ability: Anyone.
Materials: Calculators.

Starting is easy: pick any number and see how many factors it has. 13 has a fascination for some pupils because it sounds as if the answer will be a very big number. But they will probably discover that not all very big numbers have lots of factors. Calculators are needed for checking arithmetical errors. If you are basing a conjecture on the factors of 73 156 608, you need to be sure you have factorised it correctly! After some initial fun, encourage pupils to look at factors of 12 to get a feel for how factors actually arise. Do not be surprised if they do not realise that a factor k of n implies that n/k is also a factor. Let them discover this insight into the composition of numbers for themselves. If you want a lower target, try for a number with seven factors. The pupils will need to concoct some systematic way of recording their workings in order to be sure they have *all* the factors of a number. At a higher level, knowledge of permutations and combinations can simplify the situation.

7 Investigations which focus on a particular topic

The previous chapter enumerated the ways in which you might introduce a topic-related investigation into your current teaching pattern:

- **A:** Study a whole topic
- **B:** Introduce a topic
- **C:** Partially study a topic
- **D:** Follow up or extend a topic
- **E:** Practise or consolidate a skill or concept

This chapter offers you eight investigations to look at, two for each of four common topics. Each pair contains one low and one higher level of approach to the topic and in each pair the first of the problems is presented in a more structured way than the other. Suggestions, which are by no means prescriptive, are given as to the way, A–E, in which you might want to use the problems.

(1)   **Topic: Area and perimeter**

(a)   *Use* **B? C?**

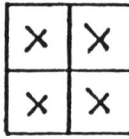

(i) This square is covered by (has area) 4 unit squares.
(ii) 4 of these squares touch the edges of the square.
(iii) The distance round the edges (perimeter) is 8 units.

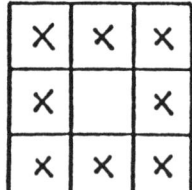

(i) This is covered by (has area) 9 squares.
(ii) 8 squares (touchers) touch the edges.
(iii) The distance round it (perimeter) is 12 units.

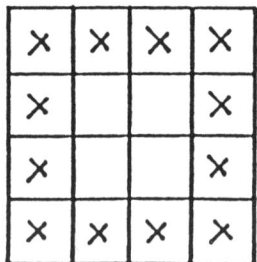

(i) The area is . . .
(ii) There are . . . touchers.
(iii) The perimeter is . . .

Can you predict the area, number of 'touchers' and perimeter for a square with sides 5 units long?

Can you predict the area, number of 'touchers' and perimeter for any square?

What is the relationship between the number of 'touchers' and the perimeter?

Can you prove your answer?

Is there any relationship between the number of 'touchers' and the area?

What about rectangles? Other shapes?

(b) *Use* **E? D?**

A class of children were working on connections between the area and perimeter of rectangles. Six children announced the following claims:

SUSAN: Any two rectangles with the same perimeter must have the same area.

DAVID: Making the perimeter of a rectangle bigger always makes the area bigger.

ALI: Every rectangle with an area of 36 square centimeters has a perimeter of at least 24 cm.

TRACY: For any particular rectangle there is another one with the same area but a bigger perimeter than before.

PAUL: Making the area of a rectangle bigger always makes the perimeter bigger.

KATIE: Any two rectangles with the same area must have the same perimeter.

Do you agree or disagree with each of these children?

Explain why in each case.

Can you come up with a similar sort of claim about the area and perimeter of rectangles?

(2) Topic: Fractions

(a) *Use* **A? E?**

Convert the following fractions to decimals:

$\frac{1}{2}, \frac{1}{3}, \frac{1}{4}, \frac{1}{5}, \frac{1}{6}, \frac{1}{7}, \frac{1}{8}, \frac{1}{9}$ (Use a calculator.)

What do you notice about some of the decimals?

Can you divide them into two categories?

Convert some more fractions such as $\frac{3}{5}, \frac{2}{9}$ etc. to decimals and see to which category they belong. Are there any which do not belong to either category? Investigate fraction families such as $\frac{1}{5}, \frac{2}{5}, \frac{3}{5}, \frac{4}{5}$.

Investigate the denominators of the fractions in each category.

Can you think of a rule which will tell you to which category a fraction belongs?

Use your rule to guess in which category you would put $\frac{1}{16}, \frac{5}{12}, \frac{1}{18}, \frac{3}{20}$.

Check with your calculator. Try guessing for some other fractions.

(b) *Use* **E? D?**

$$\frac{3}{5} = \frac{1}{3} + \frac{1}{5} + \frac{1}{15}$$
$$\frac{4}{9} = \frac{1}{3} + \frac{1}{9}$$
$$\frac{173}{340} = \frac{1}{4} + \frac{1}{5} + \frac{1}{17}$$

Investigate which fractions less than 1 can be written as the sum of different unit fractions.

(3) Topic: Square numbers

(a) *Use* **B?**

Look at this sequence of patterns:

```
*       *  *       *  *  *
        *  *       *  *  *
                   *  *  *
```

Draw the next two patterns in the sequence.

Draw the tenth pattern.

Can you find a rule to predict any pattern in the sequence?

Investigate this sequence:

```
*        *  *       *  *  *
         *  *       *  *  *
         *          *  *  *
            *  *    *  *  *
                    *  *  *
```

Investigate this sequence, too:

```
                    *
         *          *  *  *
*  *  *  *    *  *  *  *  *
```

Can you see any connection between the sequences?

(b) *Use* **E?**

In search of square numbers.

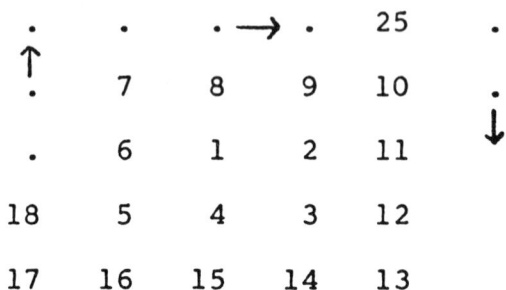

```
  .        .      . ──→ .    25      .
  ↑
  .        7      8      9    10      .
  .        6      1      2    11      ↓
 18        5      4      3    12
 17       16     15     14    13
```

Is there a pattern of square numbers emerging?

Will it continue?

If so, how? If not, why? Test and prove your conjecture.

Investigate this pattern:

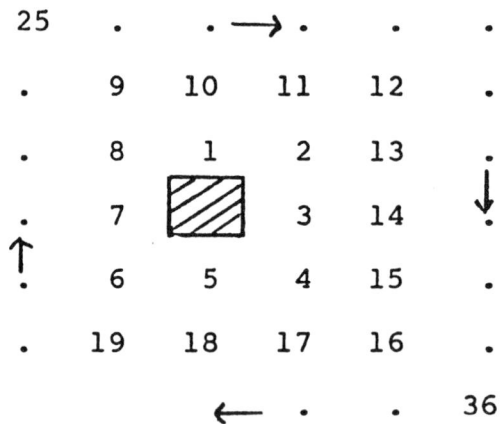

```
 25     .       . ──→ .      .      .
  .     9      10    11     12      .
  .     8       1     2     13      .
  .     7     [////]   3     14     ↓
  ↑                                 .
  .     6       5     4     15      .
  .    19      18    17     16      .
              ←──   .      .     36
```

Investigate other blockings and number spirals which yield patterns of square numbers.

(4)   **Topic: Pythagoras' theorem**

(a)   *Use* **C?**

A diagonal is drawn on a square tile making a shaded right-angled triangle: see the top of page 43.

Can you draw a square on each of the triangle's three sides? (Two are drawn to help you.)

42

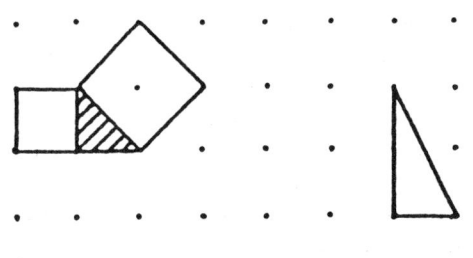

'2 by 1' triangle

Can you see any connections between the squares? Think about their areas.

Investigate the squares drawn on the sides of the '2 by 1' triangle shown.

Investigate some other triangles of your own.

(b)   *Use* **D**?
Pythagoras' theorem states that 'The square on the hypotenuse of any right-angled triangle is equal to the sum of the squares on the other two sides.'

Investigate triangles on the sides of a right-angled triangle.

Investigate other polygons or shapes on the sides of a right-angled triangle.

● **Activity 7.1**
Do it now!

Pick one of the investigations which would fit in with the topic teaching plan you have for one of your classes. Spend about three-quarters of an hour doing this investigation or, if it is too easy, also doing its harder partner.

Now sit back and look at your working. List the aspects of the topic which have been covered or touched upon. Decide which is the most effective way to use your investigation. Decide whether there are any aspects of the investigation which might prove to be stumbling blocks to the main topic-related aim of the investigation, such as, in topic 4, an inability to draw a square on a hypotenuse. Decide what help you will offer and how. Now plan your lesson in detail.

If at all possible, plan also to cover the same topic with a different class.

Reflection

After taking the investigation into the classroom, as you did with your previous investigation sessions, jot down your reflections based on the headings in Chapter 3 (page 17). Compare them with your previous reflections. Do you see any change in your attitudes, aptitudes and teaching style?

Appendix to Chapter 7
AREA AND PERIMETER

(a) **Doing hints**   The presentation is fairly heavily structured, but an early choice of tabulation will aid pattern-spotting. Notice how you count up the squares for area, touchers and perimeter, as this will help towards a proof of your results. For side length n, the generalised results are: area = n^2, touchers = $4n - 4$, perimeter = $4n$. However, these are not exactly what are asked for! Again you need to notice how you count unit squares when specialising for rectangles and other shapes in order to be able to generalise and prove your results.

Class presentation hints
Age and ability: First years or older, low ability pupils.
Materials: Squared paper.

The vocabulary and concepts of area and perimeter can be introduced or revised through this relatively brief investigation. The processes of generalisation and seeking relationships are called for. This might be a suitable investigation to follow on from 'Borders'. If you wish the investigation to have the structure given here, then a worksheet is an ideal way to present it. You would need first to check on the pupils' knowledge of the relevant vocabulary. Alternatively you might have an introductory class discussion and actually manipulate some sort of tiles. You need, too, to think what level of proof you are expecting. In a simple investigation such as this, leave pupils to devise their own recording systems, suggesting a structure only if really necessary. Later discussion on their methods would then be appropriate.

(b) **Doing hints** One counter-example is sufficient to disprove any claim, but even several positive examples do not constitute a demonstration of the overall truth of a statement. A central idea in this exploration is that a square is a special kind of rectangle. Think about maximum and minimum conditions on area and perimeter. Does multiplication always make larger?

When looking for methods of proving true statements, consider graphical representations or methods of construction if algebra or calculus fail you.

Class presentation hints
Age and ability: Bright third years upwards.
Materials: Squared paper.

Your aim will probably be to build and consolidate firm concepts of area and perimeter and of the relationship between linear and square measurement. The spin-off will be some real increase in the understanding of the nature of proof and counter-example, not to mention some splendid discussion. At a sixth form level, the exploration of methods of proof might in fact be your aim. Do your pupils realise that a rectangle can be square? The idea of the power of one example to disprove but not to prove a theory will be new to many. You may wish this to emerge from the work, however, rather than be presented formally. At the sixth form level the variety of methods of proof, their validity and level of generality, can be used to give insight to the use of graphs and calculus. This is certainly an activity at any level to be done in pairs or groups. Encourage the writing of explorations in natural language as well as in mathematical symbols.

FRACTIONS

(a) **Doing hints**   A very structured presentation – no further hints needed.

Class presentation hints
Age and ability: First to third years.
Materials: Calculators; small-squared paper; possibly a micro.

At a very basic (but nonetheless legitimate and valuable) level you may wish to use this investigation primarily to give practice in button-punching or conversely in mental division. Recurring decimals could be introduced this way or greater understanding gained of the relationships between numerators, denominators, size of fractions and their decimal equivalents. A structured presentation such as this lends itself to individual work from a worksheet. Check the vocabulary of fractions: denominator, etc. Pupils who do not know the word 'recurring' may choose categories such as 'long' and 'short' decimals. Unless you are using the problem to introduce the idea of recurrence, leave them with these headings. Later ask, 'To which category do $\frac{1}{16}$, $\frac{1}{32}$, $\frac{1}{100000}$ belong?' to introduce an idea of finite and unending decimals. Since to 7 or fewer decimal places $\frac{1}{7}$ is not obviously recurring, pupils may argue for 3 groups: finite, recurring, non-recurring. Do not correct them – wait and see whether they spot something when exploring the family of $\frac{1}{7}$. Encourage pupils to first discuss and then write down their rules. You may find that small-squared paper will encourage pupils to write down their decimals with corresponding place values one below another. This may help them to see interesting number patterns among the families.

(b) **Doing hints** Think of how decimal expansions of numbers are arrived at: in effect you are asking a series of questions, 'How many $\frac{1}{10}$s?' 'How many $\frac{1}{100}$s?' etc. Try asking instead the questions, 'How many $\frac{1}{2}$s?' 'How many $\frac{1}{3}$s? $\frac{1}{4}$s?', etc.

For example $\frac{4}{11}$. How many $\frac{1}{2}$s? – none.

How many $\frac{1}{3}$s? – one. (How can you use your calculator for a quick way to answer at this stage?)

So $\frac{4}{11} = \frac{1}{3} + \frac{(12-11)}{(11 \times 3)} = \frac{1}{3} + \frac{1}{33}$.

If you work systematically, questioning in this way, will you always eventually get a unit fraction $1/N$ such that the given fraction $p/q = 1/N + \ldots$?

Try $\frac{2}{7}$. Is it greater than $\frac{1}{2}$? $\frac{1}{3}$? $\frac{1}{4}$?

Try $\frac{3}{5}$ using this systematic approach. What do you notice?

Suppose you make a mistake when selecting your largest unit fraction. For example $\frac{3}{5}$:

Does it contain $\frac{1}{2}$? No.

Does it contain $\frac{1}{3}$? No.

Does it contain $\frac{1}{4}$? Yes.

So $\frac{3}{5} = \frac{1}{4} + \frac{(12-5)}{(5 \times 4)} \ldots$ (Complete this expansion).

What do you notice about expansions for $\frac{3}{5}$?

Can you include *any* unit fraction in your sum?

Expand $\frac{2}{11}$, $\frac{2}{17}$, $\frac{2}{73}$ systematically. What do you notice?

Can you generalise for $\frac{2}{n}$?

Which fractions can be expanded to sums of unit fractions?

Which fractions can be expressed as the sum of two unit fractions? Are these expansions unique?

Class presentation hints

Age and ability: Sixth form, post O-level fifth form.

Materials: Possibly calculators.

Looked at from an Egyptian point of view it has historical interest. It certainly highlights ideas of nested fractions and specialisation as a strategy for solving numerical problems. Discussion of the generalisations will sharpen understanding of rational numbers. A general class exploration on the lines of the 'Doing hints' is probably the best way in. Even at sixth form level fraction-strips have been found useful. Whether the pupils then work in pairs or continue to explore the problem all together is really dependent on class size and inclination. It is not at present on any A-level syllabus but . . .

SQUARE NUMBERS

(a) **Doing hints** The title gives this problem away! Try looking at the second and third sequences in different geometrical and numerical ways and produce appropriate algebraic representations.

Class presentation hints

Age and ability: First to fourth years.

Materials: Squared or spotted paper.

Two levels of approach here. If you do not use the given title then the investigation can be used to introduce or revise work on square numbers by relating geometric patterns to numbers. Ask the pupils to relate the second and third sequences to patterns of squares. They should talk to each other about what they see in the patterns. For pupils with some feeling for algebraic representation, generalisations of what they see in these sequences of patterns can be put together in a whole-class feedback session to throw up equivalences such as

$$(n+1)^2 - 1 = (n+2)n = (n+2)^2 - 2(n+2)$$

which are seen intuitively to be the same and by algebraic manipulation can be shown to be identical. If the aim is to discover square numbers then a worksheet with no preamble works well for the first sequence. Do not be surprised that some pupils do not rapidly spot the pattern. Some class discussion of ways of looking at the other sequences could then precede further individual or pair work. For older pupils you may well have to nudge them from seeing the pattern generalisation, to writing it in words and then symbols. If this can be done individually without discussion, the value of later class-together work will be greater.

(b) **Doing hints**   Here, the investigation reverses the approach to square numbers by looking at where the numbers occur in a spiral pattern. Use geometrical arguments to explain the patterns. Think about distances and directions travelled on the spiral between two consecutive square numbers. Relate this (algebraically?) to the difference between square numbers. For any rectangular, $n \times m$ block can you predict where the pattern of square numbers will start and its direction? What about L-shaped blocks?

Class presentation hints
Age and ability: First to third years.
Materials: Squared paper.

This is a good investigation for encouraging pupils to 'talk mathematics'. This in fact might be your main aim. Start with individual work to enable everyone to 'see' the patterns and lead in to discussion during which pupils are forced to use geometric language (diagonal, vertical, perimeter, etc.) to explain their ideas. It gives lots of scope for conjecturing and verifying.

PYTHAGORAS' THEOREM

(a) **Doing hints**   The title says it all (for you, not the pupils) but 'do' the investigation anyway before giving it to a class, to help you anticipate some of their problems. Can you draw a square on any line drawn from a corner to a corner on squared paper? Can you show that the theorem only applies to right-angled triangles?

Class presentation hints
Age and ability: First to third years.
Materials: Squared paper; set squares; rulers.

Obviously the primary aim is to notice that the area of the square on the hypotenuse is the same as the sum of the areas of the other two squares. Alongside this, there will be increased understanding of the properties of squares and triangles as the pupils try to make the necessary drawings. Before embarking on the investigation it would be wise to check that everyone has the properties of a square at the forefront of their minds, including less obvious facts such as 'diagonals are of equal length and at 45 degrees to the sides' and that 'diagonals of any rectangle halve its area'. If you demonstrate, using a squared OHP transparency or squared board, how to draw a square on any corner-to-corner line, you may avoid confusions which detract from the investigation. You might even want to insert the question:

Can you draw squares with each of these lines as one side? What are the areas of these squares? (Use one paper square as a unit of area.)

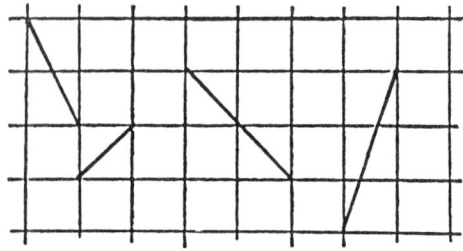

46

If pupils are to find satisfaction in making and testing hypotheses then they should not be encouraged to jump to conclusions on the basis of one or two examples. This investigation is worth spending time on, since it gives a real feel for the theorem if enough examples are explored, including, particularly, some non-right-angled triangles. Very little further teaching would be needed other than to relate geometric squares with squared numbers and hence with the numerical properties of the theorem.

(b) **Doing hints**   One approach is to stay with the squared paper and area methods used in the previous investigation. Try different-sized right-angled triangles with their bases on the sides of your right-angled triangle. Try isosceles triangles with height equal to base, or equilateral triangles, on the sides of right-angled triangles. What about unit-height rectangles? Other rectangles? Semi-circles?

Class presentation hints
Age and ability: Sixth form, bright fifth years.
Materials: Squared paper; possibly construction instruments.

Your aim will be somewhere between 'playing with Pythagoras' and (if you use a proof by reduction of polygons to squares) 'understanding the concept of area in a plane'! Spin-offs will certainly include an improved 'vision' of shapes and their related areas. Starting from nowhere is HARD. The pupils would do better to play with the previous investigation first to get the feel for drawing and calculating/counting areas. You might, even so, want to give them a few guidance hints. Remember that the given 'Doing hints' indicate only one way of tackling the problem. You or your students may well develop a quite different approach.

8 Recording and writing-up

This chapter is concerned with *recording* – keeping track of what you have done during an investigation – and *writing up* – presentation of your working for others to read. The distinction between these two will become clearer during the chapter. First, however, consider the following problem.

Problem 8.1
Frogs

An equal number of square and round counters are placed on a strip like this:

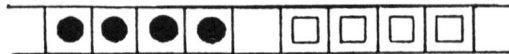

Round counters can move one place to the right *or* hop over one square counter to the right. Square counters can move one place to the left *or* hop over one round counter to the left.

Can you, by a sequence of moves, get the round counters to where the square counters start and the square counters to where the round counters start?

Activity 8.1
Do it now!

Explore the problem 'Frogs'. The important activity on this occasion is, while playing, to devise a method of recording your moves on paper. Even if you do not succeed in solving the problem, record your actions with the counters.

The investigation 'Frogs' has been chosen here to create for you a situation in which pupils often find themselves: needing a means of expression which is not yet to hand. This may happen to you only rarely since you probably have ready recourse to algebra, graphs, tabulation, etc. There is, however, no obvious way of representing frog-moves. Unlike you in this situation, pupils are not often told to invent their own notations. Standard methods are presented to them for use. If these are not really appropriate to the pupil's stage of development and need, confusion and deep-rooted misunderstanding can result.

Interpreting the problem

Before discussing various recording methods used by you and other teachers working on 'Frogs' it is actually worth looking at precisely how you interpreted the problem statement. How and what you recorded will be directly dependent upon this.

(i)   Were you concerned with the number of moves you made in order to interchange the counters? Did you find the minimum number of moves? the only number of moves? a possible number of moves?

(ii) Did you investigate the order of moves with respect to the shape of the counters? with respect to left and right movement?

(iii) Was your interest directed towards the type of move: slide or jump?

(iv) Did you focus attention on what happened to the blank space between the counters?

(v)   Were the counters each treated as individuals, labelled and a record kept of precisely what happened to each one?

Recording schemes

It is highly likely that you had not until now realised there were so many interpretations! Now try to record this sequence of moves using your scheme.

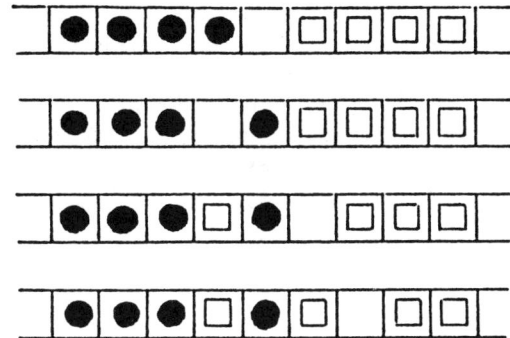

Was your scheme adequate for the task? Below are six different ways of recording the first three moves in the above sequence. Obviously a seventh method would be the pictorial record used to give you the problem. Perhaps you had an eighth way.

A   R R R R . S S S S
          R R R . R S S S S
          R R R S R . S S S
          R R R S R S . S S

B   Slide round
          Jump square
          Slide square

C

D   SJS

E   1 2 3 4 ⑤ 6 7 8 9
          1 2 3 ⑤ 4 6 7 8 9
          1 2 3 6 4 ⑤ 7 8 9
          1 2 3 6 4 7 ⑤ 8 9

F   1   2   3   4   5   6   7   8   9

| R | R | R | R | | S | S | S | S |

$R_4 \longrightarrow 5$
$S_1 \curvearrowright 4$
$S_2 \longrightarrow 6$

Some of the schemes have the merit of brevity, some that of clarity. For example D tells you nothing about which counters were moved, only the pattern of their moves; E gives the precise location of each counter but no record of slide or jump. Do you really need all the information given in the laborious recording system F? Which of these records defines a unique sequence of moves?

Look at the list of possible ways of interpreting the investigation and decide which of the recording methods would be most appropriate in each case.

What is evident from all of this is that the tool you need to use is dependent on the task in hand.

So far the focus has been on recording and not on writing up. Recording is for private working. It is to enable you to reconstruct your actions or thinking. It is not primarily for communication to others. The emphasis on pupils' work, however, is almost always on public presentation. Algorithms are taught which are not in fact appropriate to the pupils' mathematical thinking but which do give a way of 'writing it down'. Consider the calculation 'Take 39 from 71.' The standard way of writing this is

$$\begin{array}{r} 71 \\ -39 \\ \hline \end{array}$$

There then follows some form of 'borrowing' or 'paying back' symbolised by

$$\begin{array}{r} {}^6\!\!\not7{}^1\!1 \\ -39 \\ \hline \end{array} \quad \text{or} \quad \begin{array}{r} 7{}^1\!1 \\ -3\,9 \\ \hline \end{array}$$

accompanying a mental patter such as 'Nine from one won't go, so borrow one from the seven and make it six, nine from eleven is two and three from six is three'. Stop. Think. Is this really the way you would do the calculation in your head? It is far more likely that your mental patter would be on the lines of 'Thirty-nine to forty is one. Forty to seventy is thirty, so thirty-one plus one more gives 32.'

But how would you react to the following piece of pupil work?

$$39 + 1 = 40 + 30 = 31 + 1 = 32$$

The answer is right, but most mathematics teachers would be unhappy about the 'working'. Yet, if challenged, the pupil could legitimately reply, 'That is *my* recording. *I* know what it means.' This distinction between recording to aid private thinking and writing up for public communication is an important one. Too little emphasis is placed on the former, but if your teaching aims are to encourage original mathematical thinking then you must create an atmosphere where personal recording is totally acceptable. It should be made clear to pupils when a special write-up for your benefit is called for. Investigations are about exploring, trial and ERROR, gaining understanding from journeys down blind alleys, so writing-up is rarely an appropriate activity until stage 4 (see chapter 4, page 25)– if then! Talking or demonstrating might be a more relevant way of communicating. It is not being suggested here that everyone must re-invent the wheel. Offer your pupils the possibilities of using graphs, tables or diagrams but allow them to reject these formal methods of recording if they wish. Above all, allow them to invent their own algebra. You may find that as pupils become involved in investigations they actually want to communicate their work in some semi-permanent form such as a wall display for their peers. One method of encouraging them to evaluate their own work is to present each pupil with a sheet of A4 paper and ask for a display sheet on any aspect of their investigation that they consider interesting or important.

There are, nonetheless, occasions when you will want your pupils to communicate their mathematics in a more formal way. The most common reason is for assessment purposes – this is a necessary evil! Although Chapter 10 deals with ways of assessing investigative work, it is appropriate to look at ways of writing-up here. Writing about doing mathematics may well be a totally unfamiliar activity for your pupils and so, at least to start with, 'saying' should come first. This can be whole-class discussion if it really is the pupils who are doing all the talking. Probably more valuable, however, in that it involves even the less articulate members of the class, is talking through what has been done with another pupil.

Writing-up

Initially you may want to give pupils some guidelines on the structure of a write-up. This might be in the form of five questions:

- What was the problem about?
- How did you get started?
- What ideas did you have?
- Did you find anything out?
- Why did it work?

Alternatively, you might suggest they use the process list (given in Chapter 4, page 26) to aid their recall. Do not be disappointed if pupils' first attempts are rather inadequate. Go back to encouraging them to talk in pairs and then write down *what they have said*. You may well meet cries of 'But I do not know how to write it in mathematics!' because all their past experience is that 'Writing maths is about numbers and signs and things, not words.' Persevere. You are giving them a valuable skill.

A completely different way of presenting your working to others is a form of structured recording. This involves writing about what you are doing while you are actually doing it, rather than while reflecting afterwards on what you have done: in other words, producing a written running commentary alongside your investigative working. This is probably harder than the previous suggestion, but for able and experienced investigators it provides far greater insight into their thinking. If, during the reflection stage, they are encouraged to analyse their commentary in terms of process, then they are being shown a way to think about their thinking. For those who are really interested in mathematics this is a very valuable skill. An example of one student's structured record is given on page 52. The clouds on the left were the result of subsequent reflection.

Activity 8.3 **Do it now!**	Go back to your exploration of Frogs and do a brief write-up of what you did and found out, to give yourself a feel for the sorts of things on which you would want your pupils to comment.

Activity 8.4 **Do it now!**	Consider the extension to the Frogs problem in which you have dissimilar numbers of square and round counters. Play with this extension, but while doing so have a go at a structured recording on the lines of the Fibonacci example. When you have gone as far as you wish, reflect on the working and thinking you have recorded. An alternative extension might be to vary the initial number of spaces between the counters.

Activity 8.5 **Do it now!**	Finally, prepare a lesson with one of your classes in which the pupils will explore Frogs and then for homework attempt a write-up of what they did. If you pick a sixth-form group to work with, then you might prefer to get them to try a structured recording.

Fibonacci

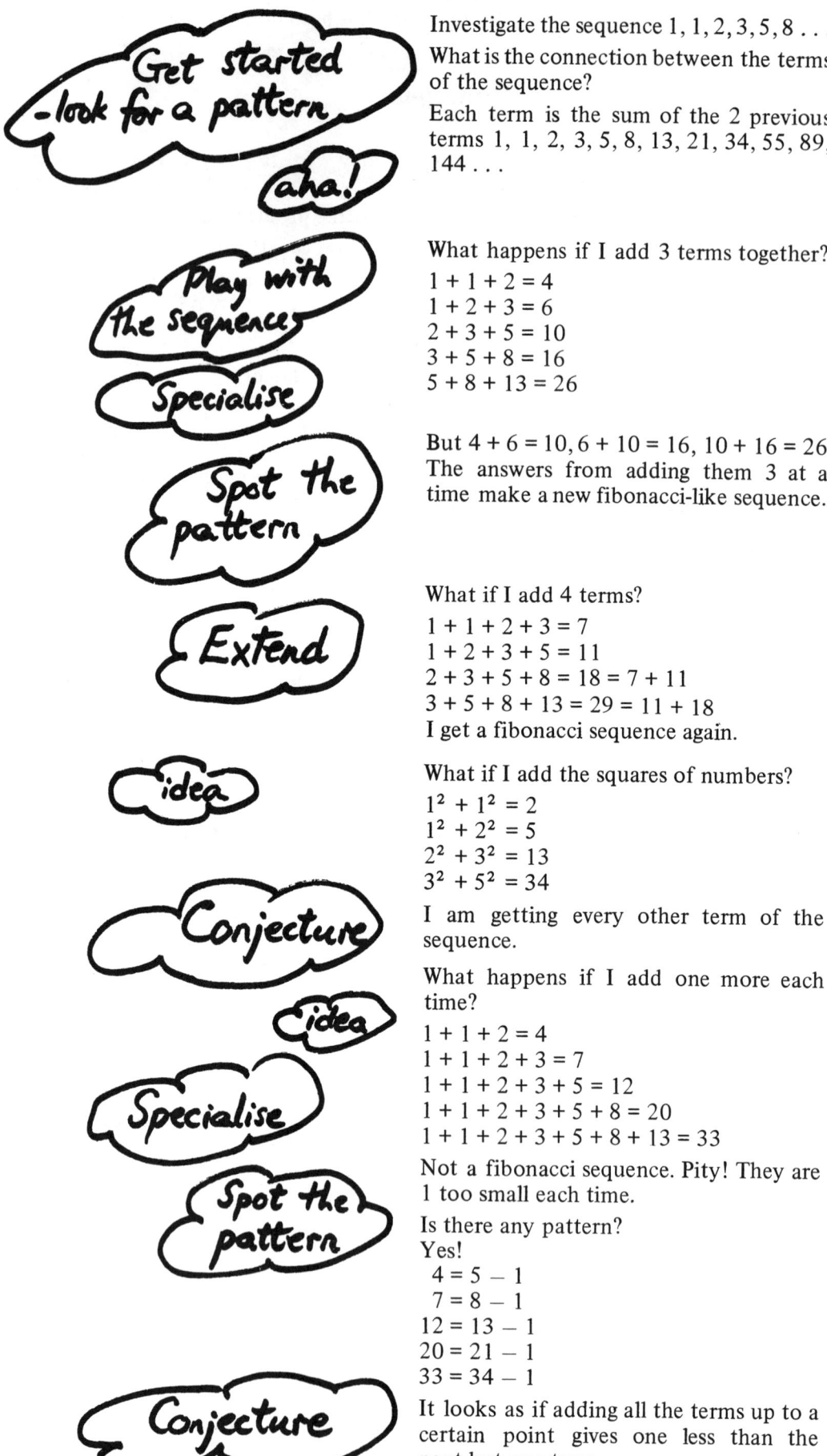

Investigate the sequence 1, 1, 2, 3, 5, 8 . . .

What is the connection between the terms of the sequence?

Each term is the sum of the 2 previous terms 1, 1, 2, 3, 5, 8, 13, 21, 34, 55, 89, 144 . . .

What happens if I add 3 terms together?

$1 + 1 + 2 = 4$
$1 + 2 + 3 = 6$
$2 + 3 + 5 = 10$
$3 + 5 + 8 = 16$
$5 + 8 + 13 = 26$

But $4 + 6 = 10, 6 + 10 = 16, 10 + 16 = 26$ The answers from adding them 3 at a time make a new fibonacci-like sequence.

What if I add 4 terms?

$1 + 1 + 2 + 3 = 7$
$1 + 2 + 3 + 5 = 11$
$2 + 3 + 5 + 8 = 18 = 7 + 11$
$3 + 5 + 8 + 13 = 29 = 11 + 18$
I get a fibonacci sequence again.

What if I add the squares of numbers?

$1^2 + 1^2 = 2$
$1^2 + 2^2 = 5$
$2^2 + 3^2 = 13$
$3^2 + 5^2 = 34$

I am getting every other term of the sequence.

What happens if I add one more each time?

$1 + 1 + 2 = 4$
$1 + 1 + 2 + 3 = 7$
$1 + 1 + 2 + 3 + 5 = 12$
$1 + 1 + 2 + 3 + 5 + 8 = 20$
$1 + 1 + 2 + 3 + 5 + 8 + 13 = 33$

Not a fibonacci sequence. Pity! They are 1 too small each time.

Is there any pattern?
Yes!

$4 = 5 - 1$
$7 = 8 - 1$
$12 = 13 - 1$
$20 = 21 - 1$
$33 = 34 - 1$

It looks as if adding all the terms up to a certain point gives one less than the next-but-one term.

Suppose I have a different series, like
4, 4, 8, 12, 20, 32, 52, 84 . . .

4 + 4 + 8 = 16	= 20 − 4
4 + 4 + 8 + 12 = 28	= 32 − 4
4 + 4 + 8 + 12 + 20 = 48	= 52 − 4
4 + 4 + 8 + 12 + 20 + 32 = 80 = 84 − 4	

For this sequence, it is 4 less.

What about
5, 5, 10, 15, 25, 40, 65 . . .

5 + 5 + 10 = 20	= 25 − 5
5 + 5 + 10 + 15 = 35	= 40 − 5
5 + 5 + 10 + 15 + 25 = 60 = 65 − 5	

This time it is 5 less.

It is always less by the first number.

Try a different sequence.
1, 2, 3, 5, 8 . . .

1 + 2 + 3 = 6	= 8 − 2
1 + 2 + 3 + 5 = 11	= 13 − 2
1 + 2 + 3 + 5 + 8 = 19	= 21 − 2

It ought to be 1 less, but it is 2 less.

Try
1, 3, 4, 7, 11, 18, 29, 47 . . .

1 + 3 + 4 = 8	11 − 3
1 + 3 + 4 + 7 = 15	18 − 3
1 + 3 + 4 + 7 + 11 = 26	29 − 3

It is always less by the *second* number, not the first. In the first few I tried, the first and second numbers were the same. Is there a way of writing *any* fibonacci-type sequence?

If a and b are the starting terms of a fibonacci-type sequence, the sequence is $a, b, a + b, a + 2b, 2a + 3b, 3a + 5b, 5a + 8b, 8a + 13b$ . . .

The 'real' fibonacci numbers are turning up as the coefficients of a and b in the new sequence.

If I call the real fibonacci terms F_1, F_2, F_3 . . .

then the sequence can be written as $a, b, F_1 a + F_2 b, F_2 a + F_3 b, F_3 a + F_4 b, F_4 a + F_5 b, F_5 a + F_6 b$ . . .

Let any sequence be represented by

$u_1, u_2, u_3, u_4, u_5, u_6$ . . .

the general term is then

$u_n = F_{(n-2)} a + F_{(n-1)} b$

for a fibonacci-type sequence.

Appendix to Chapter 8

FROGS

Doing hints   This is a classic example of the sort of investigation where specialising to small numbers or simple situations is the best starting strategy. Decide what you want to find out and start with 1-a-side. Recording your moves will help you spot patterns in the play. When you have tackled the extension to groups of n and m counters, plot 'number of moves' against 'm' for a fixed value of n. Do this for different values of n on the same set of axes. What is the significance of -1? What happens in the game when the number of spaces changes?

Class presentation hints

Age and ability: Anybody.

Materials: Counters in two shapes or colours and appropriate squared paper, or pegs in two colours and boards, or people! Squared or lined paper for recording.

Not an investigation to do from a worksheet. This is a dynamic problem, so use materials. Round and square counters work well on an overhead projector. How about two teams of 4 or 5 people sitting in a row with an empty chair between them? However you choose to present the problem, do it with at least 4 in each team. This will illustrate the rules of the game, but also show that false moves lead to an impasse and a need to start all over again! Trying to remember what they did, that led to this situation, will probably strongly indicate to your pupils the need to record. Do not suggest a way of recording, but encourage them to create their own. Working in pairs is probably the best way of approaching the problem. Many pupils will initially see 'Frogs' as a competitive game for two. It is not. On the contrary, it is a cooperative game. Let them discover this for themselves. Some will still want to talk about winning, if so get them to articulate what their 'extra' rules are: taking it in turns to move? last person to move wins/loses? person who can make the most consecutive moves wins?, etc.

A word of warning: don't expect too much from them if this is their very first attempt at writing-up, although you might have some pleasant surprises. A method of recording which is unlikely to occur to your pupils, is to plot 'number of moves' against 'number of counters on each side'. This might be an excellent opportunity to introduce them to graphs as a means of recording. With able older pupils, graphing the extensions will challenge their understanding of generalisation and prediction beyond the concrete example and into abstract mathematics.

9 Investigations involving practical working

One of the elements which the Cockcroft committee felt should be more prevalent in mathematics lessons was practical working. Since then the debate as to the meaning of 'practical' has ranged over such diverse definitions as 'useful in adult life', 'a personal everyday problem relevant to the pupil now' and 'work which requires more than just pencil and paper'. It needs to be made clear that, in the context of this chapter, it is not practical work, as defined by either of the first two statements which is being considered but the use of practical working to aid or focus investigation. Alternative labels might be 'tangible', 'material', 'three-dimensional' or 'physical' working. The aim is to encourage pupils to seek resources which will aid their understanding of a problem. One way to help the achievement of this aim is to investigate the materials themselves. A question such as 'What shapes can you make on a pin board?' can lead into description and naming of triangles and quadrilaterals or to a discussion of circles – what *is* a circle in fact? Such an exploration could lead to using pin boards rather than paper for the investigation on dots and areas in Chapter 2. You may well have to fight the prejudice that use of concrete materials is 'babyish'. Using the apparatus itself as the focus of the investigation can make the pupils aware of the tools which are available to aid their problem-solving.

The investigations offered in this chapter have been selected because they fulfil three criteria:

    (i) they involve practical working;

   (ii) they do not make unrealistic demands on resources;

  (iii) they also present opportunities to explore personal methods of recording.

Of necessity the problems here are presented on paper, but you would be better advised to introduce them by talking and handling the materials. If you are feeling adventurous you might like to try one of these investigations in the classroom without having tried it yourself first. Let the pupils know that you have not done it. Note how this affects their behaviour. Do they feel insecure? (Do you?). Are they spurred on by the challenge? You may have to exert great self-control not to interfere with their working when you want to see what happens to your own ideas. How about doing the investigation yourself for the first time in the classroom while they are working? If you do, however, do not let them be tempted to 'copy' your 'right' way.

Activity 9.1
Do it now!

Select one (or more) of the practical investigations outlined below and prepare yourself, in whatever way you choose, to take it into your classroom. When reflecting, later, on how the lessons went, try to isolate features which were related to practical working and features which might have been provoked by your acknowledged ignorance of the work they were doing.

Problem 9.1
Six hoops

Materials: 6 hoops of the same size and some larger and smaller hoops

If you have six hoops, how many regions can you make? Record what you are doing as you go along.

Extension: what if not circles?

Problem 9.2
Brahma

Materials: A model of the Tower of Hanoi. Old-fashioned kitchen weights will do if you draw three circles on a card instead of the spikes.

Eight discs of decreasing size are placed on one spike.

The object is to get all the discs on to another spike with these rules:
   (a) only one disc may be moved at a time,
   (b) no disc may ever have a smaller one below it.
Record how you move the discs.

Extension: what if not three spikes?

Problem 9.3
Tri-squares

Materials: 2 cm squares and 2 cm equilateral triangles, paper, glue
Copy and extend this pattern sequence:

How many squares, triangles, edges and vertices are there at any stage?

Create your own tessellation of squares and triangles. Find a way to describe how the pattern is made up.

How many different tessellations can be made using these triangles and squares?

Problem 9.4
Big square, little square

Materials: 1 × 1 and 2 × 2 squares, paper, glue
The four diagrams show ways to glue squares of size 1 × 1 and 2 × 2 together along their edges to make repeating patterns.

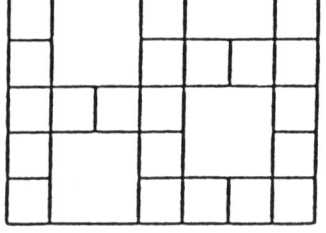 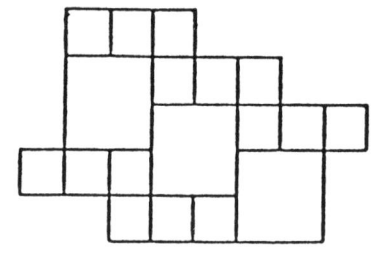 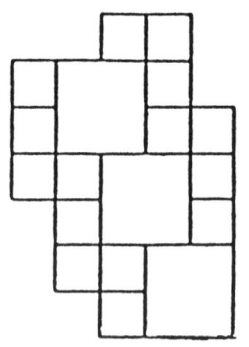 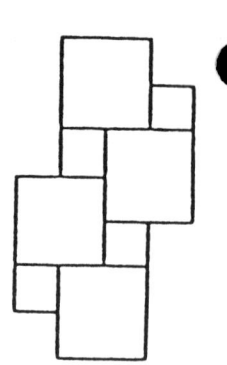

Continue the patterns.

What is the rule for continuing each pattern?

Convince someone that your rule will work.

How many other ways can you find to create repeating patterns with these shapes?

56

Develop a notation to enable you to describe any pattern unambiguously.

Extensions: What if not 1 x 1 and 2 x 2 squares?

What if not squares?

Problem 9.5
Deltahedra

Materials: equilateral triangles in stiff card (ATM produce excellent ones and also other shapes), Copydex glue – this allows you to re-use the triangles

A deltahedron is made up entirely of equilateral triangles. The rule is that each side of each triangle must be glued to one and only one other triangle.

Can you make a deltahedron from exactly 11 triangles? Can you make a general statement about the construction of deltahedra and the number of triangles needed?

Given a fixed number of triangles, how many different deltahedra can be made?

Can you make a deltahedron with a hole in it? How many triangles do you need?

Can every vertex be surrounded by the same number of triangles? What happens then?

Record what you are doing from time to time.

Extension: What if not triangles?

Problem 9.6
Families of hoops

Materials: 4 hoops of the same size, several others of different sizes, plain paper, compasses, rulers

Two hoops can be placed on the floor,

like this: or like this:

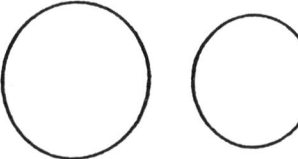
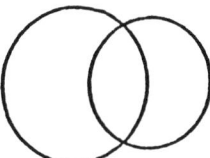

How many other different ways can they be placed in relation to each other?

What about three hoops . . . or four hoops?

Develop a means of describing each situation succinctly.

Does the size of the hoops matter?

Extension: What if not circular hoops? What about square ones?

Problem 9.7
Pyramids

Materials: lots of cubes, isometric and squared paper

The pyramids of ancient Egypt were built by piling up layer upon layer of cubical blocks of stone. The builders started with a square base and each layer was begun one block farther in than the layer below.

Build some pyramids for yourself. Record how many cubes are needed for each pyramid.

How many cube faces are visible for each pyramid?

How many faces are not visible?

Extensions: consider other constructions built in a similar way.
Try this: or this:

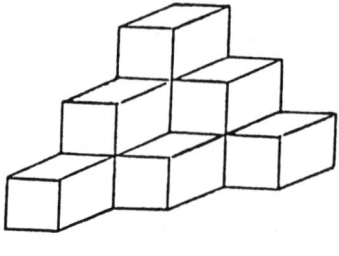 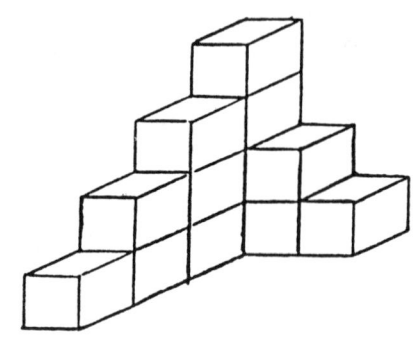

**Problem 9.8
Knots**

Materials: 2 different kinds of thick string or rope in 80–100 cm lengths, plain paper, overhead projector

A piece of string on an overhead projector produces this image:

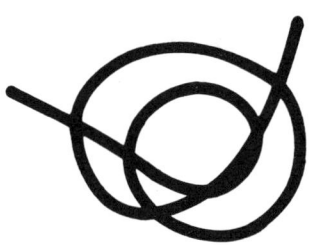

The string could be lying like this:

What other arrangement of the string would produce the same image?

Which ones would make a knot if the ends were pulled?

Devise a way of describing your string figures and investigate other knots and loops.

Extension: what if not one piece of string?

**Problem 9.9
Transformation patterns**

Materials: appropriately-patterned tiles (semi-circle and quarter-circle)

4 tiles can be cut from

Using these tiles make as many tile-patterns as you can with transformations of the tile.

Try to describe the transformations of one tile used to create each tile-pattern, e.g.

uses one reflection.

This investigation can produce some excellent wall displays.

Problem 9.10
Building symmetries

Materials: lots of cubes, isometric and squared paper

How many symmetrical shapes can you make with five cubes placed face to face? With six cubes?

Investigate, and record your shapes.

Problem 9.11
Keeping track

Materials: 5 x 5 cm squares in stiff card. A4 paper, stiff card, scissors, rulers, compasses

Take a piece of square card. Place one edge on a straight line and rotate it along this line.
What is the path traced out by a corner (vertex)?
What is the path traced out by the centre?
Investigate rotating other shapes and record the results.

Extension: What if not a straight line?

Problem 9.12
Tumbling cube

Materials: plain cube and square graph ruling with the same length of side, dice

Mark a starting square near the middle of the paper and place the cube on it. The only move allowed is to turn the cube over one edge on to an adjacent square.

Investigate the moves which take the cube from the starting square to other squares on the paper.

Extension: Use a die instead of the plain cube. Be careful to place the die in the same orientation (e.g. 1 on top and 2 facing you) every time you take it back to the starting position.

10 Assessment

Before looking at *how* you might assess pupils' abilities and progress through the investigations they are doing, it is worth briefly reviewing *why* you assess any piece of pupil work.

Why assess?

Activity 10.1
Do it now!

Spend five minutes writing down as many reasons as you can why you or other teachers might assess work. Be honest!

Activity 10.2
Do it now!

Sort your reasons under the three headings: 'for the pupils', 'for yourself', 'for others'.

You might like to compare your list with that given in the Appendix to this chapter, which was compiled by a group of teachers on an in-service course working with the pilot version of this book.

Why investigate?

Activity 10.3
Do it now!

Return your thoughts to investigations and spend five minutes compiling a list of reasons why you are doing them with your pupils. Again, be honest! Try to group these reasons under the three headings given in the previous activity.

In order to think about the assessment of investigations these two lists need to be combined in some way. Keep them in front of you as you work through this chapter. You may find you want to add to or alter them as you go along.

What to assess

Another pause for thought is needed here. What exactly is it that you wish to assess? What exactly is it that you can assess? Is it:
  the recording?
  the results?
  the write-up?
  the thinking behind the write-up?
  the processes used?
  the mathematics learned through the investigation?
What is it that the pupils expect from your assessment? They may have personal, well-defined expectations and feel cheated or frustrated by an unexplained, unfamiliar response to their work.
  The Appendix to this chapter contains the work of two 12-year-old boys who spent a lesson playing with the problem 'Frogs' and then had the task of writing up their experience for homework. Consider the different aspects of assessment with respect to David's and Ulwyn's work.

What does the *recording* tell you? Not a lot – except that they were doing something and had devised a method of recording it. What about *results*? First you need to decide what results you are looking for. David was clearly only interested in who won the most games, which does not, however, prove that he did nothing in terms of thinking out strategies or noticing numbers and types of moves. This could only be verified by having seen the pupils in the classroom as they tackled the problem. One difficulty in applying any normal assessment procedures to investigations is immediately highlighted. So much of what goes on in the way of mathematical thinking is based on activity and is thus hard to write down. In particular, results are rarely the aim of an investigation. Watching pupils at work will frequently tell you more than any write-up about the way problems are tackled and ideas tried out. This of itself could be a reason for wishing to assess the *write-up*, not as a guide to mathematical thinking, but as an effective method of communication. Assessment can be used to focus pupils on a particular aspect of their work and David needs encouragement to sort out and write down the mathematical elements of his activities. Judged as a piece of communication, Ulwyn's write-up is excellent. You have a very clear idea of what he was doing and *thinking*.

One of the aims of investigative work is to lead children consciously towards the *processes* of mathematical thinking. One way of doing this is to assess which processes they already use in their working and which need encouragement. For instance, look at the boys' work with reference to this list of processes:

- getting started
- specialising
- organising
- conjecturing
- checking
- generalising
- proving

The problem was initially tackled by the whole class, but Ulwyn and David used the strategy of simplifying and specialising to get themselves involved. The ability to organise their working is shown in Ulwyn's write-up by the systematic way in which they tried first 1, then 2, then 3 counters on each side. The last two lines of the write-up reveal that Ulwyn is beginning to conjecture, and even tentatively to generalise.

No assessment can be made of the *mathematics learned* during the investigation since 'Frogs' does not contain any specific mathematical content.

How to assess

Return to the question of *how* to assess investigations. Basically assessment can be classified as 'formative' or 'summative'. That is to say, its purpose is to inform with a view to affecting future work, or to make a statement about the ability of the pupil to date. For the classroom teacher this generally corresponds to your aims when assessing ordinary class work as compared with the formal assessment carried out at the end of a school year, or by GCSE and other external examining bodies.

Consider first assessing pupils' day-to-day progress through class and homework. Look at the reasons for assessment you have collected under the heading 'For others'. The category probably includes 'Parents', 'The system', 'Setting' and 'Homework records' among others. For these purposes you need a scheme providing summative assessments which is quick to operate, brief to record and has common currency of meaning. Two suggestions are that you roughly rank-order the write-ups, or, better, that you take classwork into consideration and group the pupils in, say, four groups graded A to D. Think carefully before you argue that more precise or detailed information is needed for these records.

Now consider the more important reasons for assessing pupils' work: those collected under the headings 'For the pupils' and 'For yourself'. These categories are concerned with feedback, diagnosis and motivation. You need a scheme which provides formative assessment, conveying information about what the pupils are doing, how they are progressing in their ways of thinking and the stage they have reached in their ability to communicate. Ranks or grades have no value here and comments, verbal or written, are essential. A problem arises, however, when you wish to keep a record of the pupils' progress. The following checklist and chart provide *one* method of recording. *Try* working with it before you adapt it or abandon it for some more appropriate method of recording of your own.

You need one chart for each pupil, and the idea is that, whenever you notice an event you wish to record, you enter the date in the appropriate box. Underneath the chart you record the investigation being explored. The checklist is to help you recognise the various process activities.

CHECKLIST

(a) Which of the following processes is the pupil demonstrating? Is the pupil:
   (i) **Getting started**: needing precise, directed starting suggestions; needing hints and prompts; seeing the problem after discussion with friends; spontaneously formulating a question and line of approach?
   (ii) **Specialising**: playing around the investigation with particular examples; trying out ideas?
   (iii) **Organising**: being systematic; recording results; ordering data?
   (iv) **Conjecturing**: producing an idea; guessing a pattern; predicting a result?
   (v) **Checking**: trying out a conjecture with specific examples (specialising again); trying more general checks?
   (vi) **Generalising**: extending a conjecture to a general statement about the problem; predicting a generality?
   (vii) **Proving**: Convincing herself; convincing others; rigorously proving?

(b) At what level is the pupil communicating the mathematics which is going on? Is the pupil:
   (i) **Seeing**: 'Aha!'; spotting; doing?
   (ii) **Saying**: *what* the problem is about; commenting on what she is doing; explaining what she thinks is happening?
   how she is tackling the investigation; what gave rise to the ideas and conjectures?
   why she is specialising in a particular way; why she believes in the conjecture; convincing a friend; persuading a foe?
   (iii) **Recording**: writing down jottings and results as she goes along; explaining the jottings on paper; writing down the 'what', 'how', and 'why' that she has said; explaining using mathematical language and symbolism; writing a convincing argument to support the conjecture; rigorously proving?

Chart 1

	Directed	Hinted	Spontaneous
Starting			
Specialising			
Organising			

	Seeing	Saying			Recording		
		What	How	Why	Jotting	Words	Mathematical Language
Conjecturing							
Checking							
Generalising							
Proving							

What are the advantages of this method of recording assessment? It is certainly quick, and does not necessarily involve taking the pupils' work in to mark. It can be used spontaneously – when you notice a pupil achieving success in some area just jot down the data. It gives a reminder to focus your attention on a particular pupil whose record sheet has not been dated recently. It illustrates progress and stagnation and is thus a prompt for help when too many dates are in one box. There is no need to record every pupil on every investigation.

On Ulwyn's chart, 'Today' records his achievements on the 'Frogs' investigation.

Chart 2
Ulwyn's chart

	Directed	Hinted	Spontaneous
Starting			9.10.85
Specialising		9.10.85	Today
Organising	26.11.85		Today

9.10.85: Happy Numbers
26.11.85: Borders
Today: Frogs

	Seeing	Saying			Recording		
		What	How	Why	Jotting	Words	Mathematical Language
Conjecturing	9.10.85	26.11.85 Today			Today		
Checking							
Generalising	26.11.85 Today						
Proving							

Formal summative assessment

The method of assessment discussed above is not really appropriate for formal occasions as it gives no guide to the production of a grade. Three alternatives are offered here.

A Judge the piece of work as a whole and give it a grade. Do not become involved in the niceties of trying to allocate marks for wild conjecturing or erroneous checking. Just get a 'feeling' for the piece of work. Ask yourself such questions as:

'Does it contain some outstanding feature?'

'Does it show a spark of originality?'

'Has the problem been extended (in an unusual way)?'

'Does the presentation have overall coherence?'

You may be surprised but encouraged to learn that groups of teachers working independently in this way on the same scripts had a considerable measure of agreement on the grades they awarded.

B If you lack confidence in this method, you might prefer to award grades dependent on the level of sophistication the pupil has reached. Suggested levels are:
1   An unanalytic record of the work-path and ideas.
2   A presentation of path, ideas and some results.
3   Some analysis of the results, e.g. notices patterns, etc.
4   Explanation of the patterns and relationships.
5   Generalisation and verification of solutions.
6   Rigorous proof of hypotheses.

C If you are forced to give numerical marks to the work you are assessing, then try forming a mark scheme based on the checklist and a combination of the following two ways of considering the work.

(a) The presentation as a means of communication:
   (i)   Is the problem clearly formulated?
   (ii) Are the lines of approach explicit?
   (iii) Is there appropriate use of diagrams and symbolisations?
   (iv) Is there discussion of interpretations, conjectures and conclusions?

(b) The mathematical depth of the work:
   (i)   the level at which the investigation is entered;
   (ii) the range and depth of extensions considered;
   (iii) the accuracy of the actual mathematics considered;
   (iv) the ability to interpret and generalise from results;
   (v)   the quality and rigour of proofs.

Activity 10.4
Do it now!

Take some of your pupils' work and try out the various assessment methods suggested.

GCSE

The assessment schemes so far suggested have been tried in the classroom and found to be workable, effective methods of assessing pupils' investigational work. Your main concern at present, however, may be ' . . . but which do I use for GCSE course work?'. There is no such thing as 'The Definitive GCSE Scheme'. Each examination board has produced its own guidelines on mark allocation for course work, some very precise, some allowing teachers a degree of autonomy. It is hoped that the questions and suggestions raised in the schemes earlier in this chapter will guide your thinking when applying a GCSE marking scheme.

And now for some light relief:

Problem 10.1
Factor chains

Take any number. Write down all its factors including 1 but excluding the number itself. Add these factors to get a new number. Write down and then add the factors of the new number. Continue.

Activity 10.5
Do it now!

Play with the investigation Factor chains. Plan it for use with a class. Include provision for the pupils to write up their experiences. See the Appendix to this chapter.

While the class is working on the problem, try to 'date' charts for a few of the pupils. When you look at their write-ups, treat it as an occasion for formal assessment and award grades by one of the two suggested methods. Do not necessarily pass these on to the pupils! This time the exercise is for your benefit, not theirs.

Appendix to Chapter 10

1 WHY ASSESS WORK?

For **pupils**: to give feedback to pupils
to diagnose their difficulties
pupils want it
encouragement – 'I got it right'
motivation – 'I have to give it in'
shows that you value the pupils' work

For **yourself**: find out what pupils can't do
find out what pupils can do
feedback on your teaching
to set individual work levels
for records you can look back on

For **others**: everything at school is assessed
parents expect it
the system expects it
political pressure
to divide classes into sets, etc.
to inform other teachers
for the records
keep other people happy you are working!

Doubtless you can add to this list.

Their joint recording:

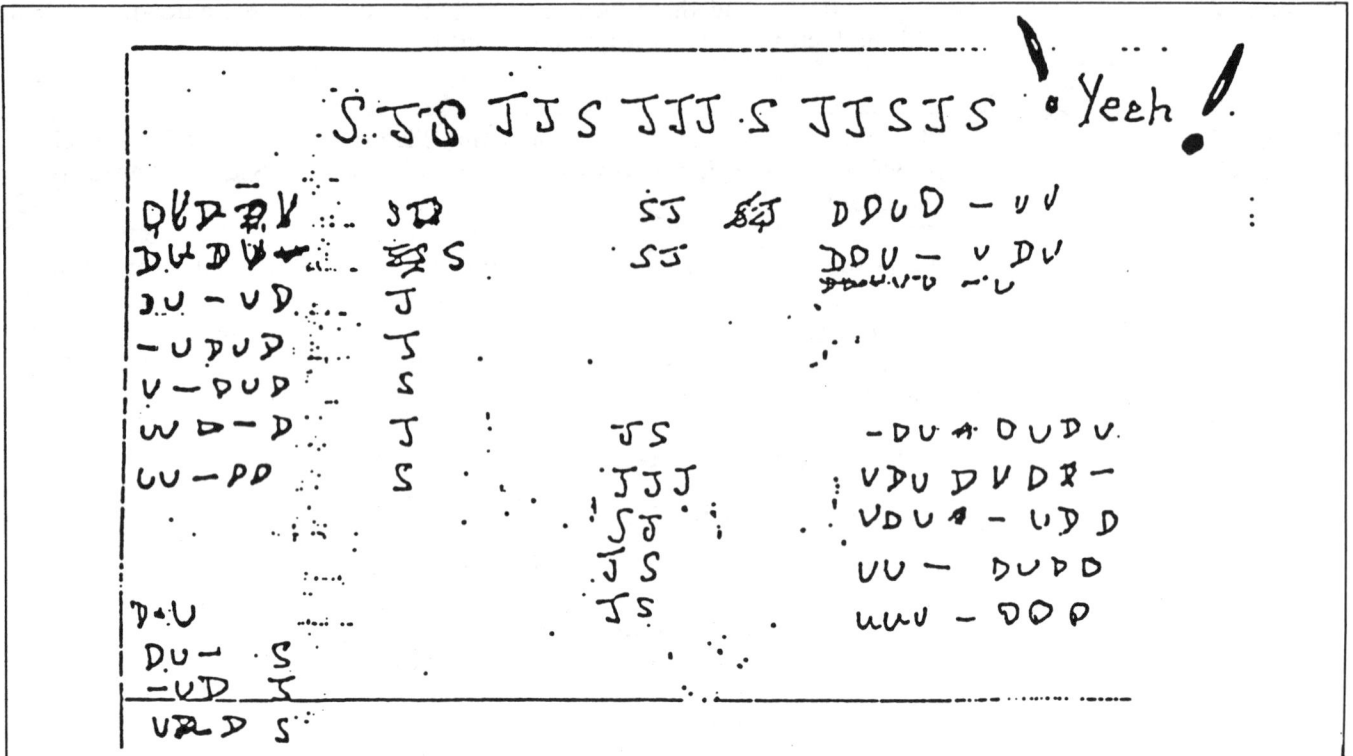

Ulwyn's write-up:

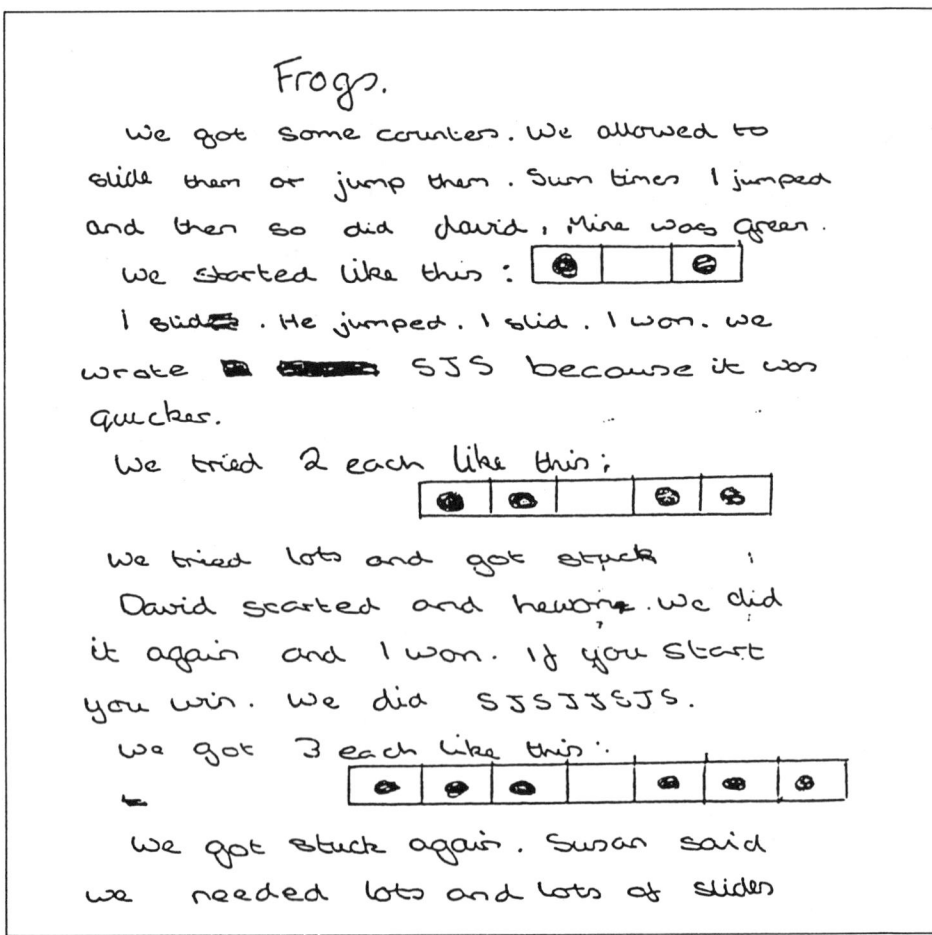

e jumps. So we did some more. I won but we had to do it again so we could write it down. We did SJSJJSJJJS JJSJS !

1 was 3

2 was 8

3 was ~~FF~~ 15

It will be more slides and jumps for 4

It will be lots more for 5 million !

David's write-up:

We started the lesson with two teams playing frogs. Anne-marie and Stephen and Simon were on one side, Ned and Rachel and Sam were on the other. Nobody won because they kept getting stuck. We had to go and play it with counters. Ulwyn won 4 and I won 1. He was lucky. I usually win.

3 FACTOR CHAINS

Doing hints Follow the instructions and you will create a chain such as $12 \to 16 \to 15 \to \ldots$ Are there any numbers which do not give rise to a chain? Can you present your results in a diagram of some form?

Class presentation hints
Age and ability: first to fifth years.
Materials: none

This might be the moment to try presenting pupils with the bald problem statement, *and no hints*. Having got over the initial shock of deciding for themselves what they are supposed to do, most pupils will be able to start. Fill in the charts for 'starting' for the pupils you have picked to assess. Encourage them to work alone on this occasion to make your task easier. Notice, but don't interfere with the recording methods the pupils adopt. You may well see such things as: $12 = 1 + 2 + 3 + 4 + 56 = 16 = 1 + 2 + \ldots$ Consult your conscience as to how to react! If you decide to interrupt and impose your recording methods, a good alternative is:

$12: 1 + 2 + 3 + 4 + 6 = 16$
$16: 1 + 2 + 4 + 8 = 15$
$15: 1 + 3 + \ldots$

Look for whether your chosen pupils work systematically or pick random starting numbers. Do they spot what happens when an existing chain is entered (conjecturing? checking?) Can they tell you about it? Can they tell you why (generalising)? Later notice what they write for homework. Does anyone try some diagrammatic representation?

11 Sixth form investigations

It is at the sixth form level that many teachers are most likely to find the demands of the syllabus, the quantity of content and the vital importance of examination results overpowering. Certainly there is no incentive to waste time on investigations. Pause. Consider again the pupils with whom you are working. In the sixth form you have those pupils who have chosen to study mathematics to a higher level, many because they are interested and fascinated by the subject. To these, least of all, should you be offering instrumental rather than relational learning – mathematical techniques rather than understanding. An ATM Sixth Form Project bulletin in 1968 stated:

> . . . the weight of tradition and the requirements of the A-level examination combined to foster the learning of a range of set techniques for solving a limited class of problems, and to discourage pupils from becoming involved in the more extensive kind of mathematical activity which is characteristic of professional mathematical work . . . . In short they (the pupils) were unaware of mathematics as an activity of people, seeing it simply as a static body of knowledge.

All too often they are shown a mathematical trick, possibly even given a demonstration of its validity and then expected to add it on to their list of knowledge and use it when required. The two questions often left unanswered are:

'What prompted someone to devise the technique in the first place?'

'How, if at all, does it fit with the understanding of mathematical concepts which I already have?'

Consider a simple but effective example. Given that the pupils are familiar with differentiation of powers and other simple functions, a next stage would be to introduce the differentiation of a product of such functions.

Problem 11.1

If u and v are two functions of x then investigate $\dfrac{d(uv)}{dx}$.

A good way to get started is to specialise: pick some functions you know how to differentiate.

If $u = x^2$ and $v = x^3$, then $uv = x^5$

$$\frac{du}{dx} = 2x \qquad \frac{dv}{dx} = 3x^2 \qquad \frac{d(uv)}{dx} = 5x^4.$$

Try other ways of splitting up x^5

Try other known functions: $x^8, x^3, \ldots$.

Can you see a way to connect $u, v, \dfrac{du}{dx}, \dfrac{dv}{dx}$ and $\dfrac{d(uv)}{dx}$? Is there a pattern?

Generalise your ideas. Can you prove them?

This small but illuminating investigation, which is probably best done individually or in pairs, can lead into a class discussion of differentiation of functions such as $(x + 3)^2$. Ask pupils to offer their conjectures as to the result of differentiating this function before multiplying out and checking by differentiation of individual terms. Do they want to revise their conjectures? What about the derivative of $(x + 3)^3$? . . . of $(x + 3)^4$? . . . of $(4x + 3)^2$?

How does their rule fit with $(x + 3)^2$?

Can they generalise?

This approach may not be very far from the way you teach the topic at the moment, but the emphasis here is on conjecturing, checking and generalising, rather than on learning the rule. Once you become familiar and confident with working with investigations you will find that, in fact, you present your teaching in many areas in a more investigative style. Pupils, too, will come to expect this approach to learning.

The possibility of a pupil pursuing and producing ideas which you had not envisaged is greater here than lower down in the school. This should not deter you. Imagine the sense of achievement, the sense of creating mathematics, available to a pupil already interested in exploring this field. Nonetheless, it does take courage to admit that you have not travelled that particular path.

Throughout this pack mention has been made of extensions to many of the investigations which are suitable at the sixth form level. These are summarised in the Appendix to this chapter. Most of them encourage sophisticated levels of mathematical thinking such as rigorous proof, non-integer solutions, broad generalisation, and even elegance. Some also relate to the content of the A-level syllabus.

Below, however, are investigations which relate specifically to four topics on that syllabus, and illustrate the different ways an investigation can be incorporated into sixth form teaching.

Topic-based investigations

Problem 11.2

A   SEQUENCES AND SERIES

(a) Use numerical methods to investigate the terms of the sequence

$$\frac{(a + b)}{(c + d)}, \frac{(2a + b)}{(2c + d)}, \ldots, \frac{(na + b)}{(nc + d)}$$

for various values of a, b, c and d, as $n \to \infty$

This explores the ideas of limiting values with real numbers before attacking the theory using algebra.

(b) Use numerical methods (a calculator or micro program will make life easier) to investigate the series

$$1 + \frac{1}{n} + \frac{1}{n^2} + \frac{1}{n^3} \ldots \text{ for specific integer values for } n.$$

What can you say about each of these series as the number of terms you calculate becomes large?

Can you generalise for $\sum \frac{1}{n^r}$ as $r \to \infty$ for any value of n?

What about non-integer values for n?

(c) Investigate $\sum \frac{1}{r}$ as $r \to \infty$.

This introduces the ideas of convergence, divergence and sums to infinity and again the numerical, rather than algebraic, treatment gives insight into 'what is really happening'.

B   CALCULUS

Problem 11.3

(a) What are the most economical (in terms of metal used) dimensions of a cylindrical can of given volume?

(b) Investigate cones which can be made from a circle of paper of radius r.

Both investigations provide a need for maximum or minimum values and hence calculus.

C   TRIGONOMETRY

Problem 11.4

Using a microcomputer, investigate the graphs of the form
$y = a \cos x + b \sin x$.

A basis for learning a standard piece of theory in trigonometry.

D   RATIONAL FUNCTIONS

Problem 11.5

Investigate the graphs of functions of the form

$$y = \frac{(x - a)(x - b)}{(x - c)(x - d)}.$$

Sketch your predictions before using a microcomputer to plot them for you.

This offers insight into rational functions and allows pupils to test their understanding with prompt feedback and opportunity to modify their ideas.

Using a microcomputer

There is much to be said for ensuring that sixth form pupils have access to standard pieces of software such as *FGP* (function graph plotter) (Shell/ITMA *Micros in the Mathematics Classroom*, Longman) or D. O. Tall, *Supergraph*, Glentop Publishing). In explorations such as C and D, the micro-computer allows the pupils to discover easily the effects of changing parameters. This would be very tedious and too time-consuming to do by hand. Similarly, it allows pupils to investigate rather than 'take on trust' the limits of functions such as $\sin \theta / \theta$ as $\theta \to 0$. It provokes the question, 'What if . . .' and enables pupils to find the answer.

A further role for investigation in the sixth form (or indeed at any stage) is to strengthen the understanding of ostensibly unrelated knowledge by constructing links and illuminating relationships between them. Two examples are given.

E   INDUCTION AND ALGEBRA

Problem 11.6

Investigate Σr^k for various fixed values of k.

Having derived the standard sums:

$$\sum r = \frac{n(n + 1)}{2} \quad \text{and} \quad \sum r^2 = \frac{n(n + 1)(2n + 1)}{6}, \quad 1 \leqslant + \leqslant n$$

evaluate $\Sigma r(r + 1)$

Generalise to Σr^k by means of the easier-to-handle series
$\Sigma r(r + 1)(r + 2) \ldots (r + k - 1)$

F   INTEGRATION AND SERIES

Problem 11.7

Investigate the relationship between $\displaystyle\sum_{r=1}^{n} \frac{1}{r}$ and the area under the graph

$y = \dfrac{1}{x}$ between $x = 1$ and $x = n$.

Generalise to the relationship between $\displaystyle\sum \frac{1}{r^k}$ and areas under the graph

$y = \dfrac{1}{x^k}$.

**Activity 11.1
Do it now!**

Choose one of the investigations A to F and explore it. Consider when you might use it with a class.

Resources

The ATM have produced two books of A-level investigations grouped by topic: *These Have Worked For Us at A-level* and *These Have Also Worked For Us At A-level*. On the whole the investigations are very structured, but do allow pupils to feel involvement in the mathematics they are striving to assimilate.

Discussion starters

Whatever the external pressures, it is good occasionally to throw a challenging mathematical statement to sixth form pupils and encourage them to discuss it. Four such provocative statements are suggested here. None are trivial and all will reveal some deeply held but possibly unhealthy concept formations.

1   What is the difference between 0.999999 . . . and 1?
2   '74 is closer to 81 than to 64, so $\sqrt{74}$ must be closer to 9 than it is to 8.' True? Generalisable? Proof?
3   A neurotic frog sitting on the bank of a circular pond wants to get to the opposite bank. He jumps half the distance, landing on a lily-pad in the centre. Fearing he will not make it to the opposite bank, he turns and jumps half the distance back to the bank he is now facing. He continues this behaviour of turning round and jumping half the distance to the bank. Will he ever make dry land again?
4   '$n^2 - n$ is always divisible by 2.
    $n^3 - n$ is always divisible by 3.
    $n^4 - n$ is always divisible by 4'
    True? Generalisable? Proof?

Appendix to Chapter 11

Investigations already mentioned

S-factors (p. 9):   think about non-integer sum-factors.
Choose a Number (p. 29):   convergence.
Painted Cube (p. 30):   binomial theorem.
Areas and Perimeters (p. 35):   rigour; elegance; non-integer solutions; extend to any shape.
Unit Fractions (p. 41):   see Appendix 7.
Area and Perimeter (b) (p. 40):   proof.
Pythagoras for any shape (p. 43):   see Appendix 7.
Fibonacci (p. 52):   difference equations.
Keeping Track (p. 59):   loci; cycloids.

A   SERIES AND SEQUENCES

(a) Doing hints   Simple specialisation essential! Concentrate to start with on the values 0 or 1 for a, b, c and d. When do you have convergence and when divergence?

Class presentation hints
Materials: Calculators; micros.

This is a valuable investigation for pupils who have already worked with standard series and sequences. It ties disparate sequences together and shows how the particular arise from the general form. Alternatively, given some structure, the investigation could act as a starting point for exploring particular series and sequences. It is worth emphasising that there are some 'forbidden' values for c and d. What are they?

(b) **Doing hints**   Evaluate $1 + \dfrac{1}{2} + \dfrac{1}{2^2} + \dfrac{1}{2^3} \ldots$ and then go on to $1 + \dfrac{1}{3} + \dfrac{1}{3^2} \ldots$ etc.

Watch or record what is happening to the sum. Try to predict the value of the sum before you turn to the calculator. (Do not calculate it using some already-known formula!) Expressing the limit of the sum as a fraction may help you to see a pattern which enables you to generalise.

Non-integer values fall into two groups (or four if you are playing with negative values): those greater than or equal to 1 and those less than 1.

Class presentation hints
Materials: Calculators; micros.

Use this investigation before doing any work on sums of GPs – possibly even before formalising GPs at all. The idea that is being offered to the pupils is that of sums in certain cases tending to a finite, knowable limit. Expressing those limits as $2, \dfrac{3}{2}, \dfrac{4}{3}, \dfrac{5}{4}$, etc. (organisation of specialising is essential here) will lead them to conjecture the limit of the sum as $\dfrac{n}{(n-1)}$.

Do not fiddle with this expression! Later when you go through the theoretical proof of sum to infinity of a GP you can relate $\dfrac{a}{(1-r)}$ back to

$$\frac{1}{1 - \dfrac{1}{n}} = \frac{n}{(n-1)}.$$

When the pupils move on to non-integer values of x, do not hint unless absolutely necessary that it is important whether $x \geqslant 1$ or $x < 1$. With luck they will stumble on this as well as the possibility of negative x.

(c) **Doing hints**   The emphasis here is on conjecture. Can you prove your answer?

Class presentation hints
Materials: Calculators

Ask for conjectures as to the behaviour of $\displaystyle\sum \dfrac{1}{r}$ before letting them calculate it. This is actually best done by hand with a calculator rather than on the micro so that conjectures may be discussed and changed as the value of r increases. The pupils' intuition will be challenged.

B   CALCULUS

Doing hints   (a) Find expressions for surface area and volume in terms of radius and height. Reduce to one variable. Differentiate. Check that it is a minimum not a maximum.

(b) Find expressions for surface area and volume in terms of θ. Consider maximum and minimum.
Remember 'r' is not a variable.

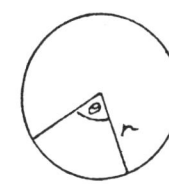

Class presentation hints
Materials: Possibly paper, scissors, glue or paper clips.

Both investigations provide practice for finding maximum and minimum values through differentiation. The modelling in (a) is simpler than that in (b). Do not suggest the hint given above for (b). The major part of the modelling problem is in deciding to base the equations on θ. Since these are both real situations, it is worth discussing the real-world implications of the results of the differentiations.

C TRIGONOMETRY

Doing hints Plot the functions for various values of a and b. Comment on what you see. Think about Pythagorean triplets: i.e. a, b, c, for which $a^2 + b^2 = c^2$.

Class presentation hints
Materials: Micros; FGP or Supergraph program.

Check that the pupils are familiar with the graphs of $\cos x$ and $\sin x$ (start with the special cases when $a = 0$ or $b = 0$?). You can drive this investigation by discussion and one micro at the front, but pupils are more likely to gain a good grasp on the subject if they experiment in pairs with the different values of a and b which seem appropriate to them. You might want to nudge them into considering $3 \cos x + 4 \sin x$ and $4 \cos x + 3 \sin x$. Does the amplitude 5 suggest any other values for a and b worth trying?

D RATIONAL FUNCTIONS OF A QUADRATIC

Doing hints Find zero values of the function and values for which it is not defined. Choose values for a, b, c, d and try to sketch the curve. What if instead of $(x - a)$ you have $(a - x)$? Extend the investigation to consider numerators or denominators of

$$x^2 + 1 \text{ and } x^2 + x + 1.$$

Class presentation hints
Materials: Micros; FGP or Supergraph

The advantage of this approach is that pupils can work and test themselves on features on the function of which they are unsure. The instant feedback available to them is invaluable.

E INDUCTION AND ALGEBRA

Doing hints Specialise to the case $k = 1$. Try specific sums, such as $1 + 2 + 3 + 4 + 5$, before attempting to justify the standard sum $\sum r = \dfrac{n(n + 1)}{2}$.

Look at the results from as many different points of view as possible, since the idea behind this investigation is that this is the progenitor of two different families:

$\Sigma r^2 = 1^2 + 2^2 + \ldots$ $\qquad$ $\Sigma r(r + 1) = 1 \times 2 + 2 \times 3 + \ldots$

$\Sigma r^3 = 1^3 + 2^3 + \ldots$ $\qquad$ $\Sigma r(r + 1)(r + 2) = 1 \times 2 \times 3 + 2 \times 3 \times 4 + \ldots$

$\qquad \Sigma r^k$ $\qquad\qquad$ $\Sigma r(r + 1)(r + 2)(r + 3) \ldots \qquad (r + k)$

Facts about series in the first column can be deduced from discoveries about series in the second column and vice versa. Surprisingly, it is the second column which is easier to handle, using a trick: each term of the series can be written as a difference of terms in the next series, e.g.

$$2 \times 3 = \frac{1}{3} (2 \times 3 \times 4 - 1 \times 2 \times 3).$$

This makes it easier to add up the terms.

Class presentation hints
Materials: None.

The value of this approach is again that it offers numerical insight to illuminate complicated expressions. If $\sum r = \dfrac{n(n + 1)}{2}$ is not yet known, then concentrate on this and aim to collect at least three different justifications from different small groups. The next step is then to encourage them to try the same method on Σr^2 or on $\Sigma r(r + 1)$ and to see the relationship between $\Sigma r(r + 1)$ and $\Sigma r^2 + \Sigma r$. Most methods, for example, 'induction', or 'express each term as a difference', work better for the second series than for the first but do not give pupils hints or algebraic tricks at too early a stage.

F   INTEGRATION AND SERIES

Doing hints   Remember that integration is a statement about area. Think about the series as another statement about area. Draw a diagram!

Class presentation hints
Materials: Graph paper.

Sixth formers are often loath to sketch or draw diagrams. 'Series' is seen as an algebraic topic. Do not draw the diagram for them but suggest that they try to represent $\int \dfrac{1}{r}$ in some graphical form. Even if they have the idea of drawing rectangles below the curve you may need to nudge them towards the possibility of drawing rectangles above the curve. Link the conclusions reached to the idea of integration as a limiting sum, particularly when they go on to consider $\dfrac{1}{r^k}$ and $y = x^k$ for $k < 1$.

DISCUSSION STARTERS

1 This challenges ideas of infinity:

$$3 \times \frac{1}{3} = 1, \quad 3 \times 0.333\ldots = 0.999\ldots = 1?$$

2 Play with calculators and pairs of squares. Proof or refutation depends on the difference between $\dfrac{(a^2 + b^2)}{2}$ and $\left(\dfrac{(a + b)}{2} \right)^2$. Consider the logic involved. Does 'A implies B' have as automatic converse as 'Not A implies not B'? This challenges ideas of proof and deduction.

3 A diagram is essential! After that, discussion to establish the kind of jumps being made provokes consideration of convergence and limiting positions.

4 A single counter-example is all that is needed to disprove a statement; the converse is, of course, not true (see discussion starter 2). Specialising to start with will often save much algebraic manipulation by throwing up a false result.

   To look for divisibility, you need to find a factorised expression. The three given statements can be easily factorised. The factors of $n^3 - n$ give the key to a solution method. This method introduces, indeed depends upon, 'proof by starting somewhere else!'.

12 15-minute fillers

How often have you had a few minutes spare at the end of a lesson? How often have you wanted to change direction for the last quarter of an hour because the pupils are flagging? The rest of this final chapter consists mainly of a collection of '15-minute fillers' appropriate for just such occasions. The criteria for inclusion were:

(i) The problem can be communicated in no more than two minutes.
(ii) There is at least one instant obvious way to get started.
(iii) Pupils will have achieved something within 15 minutes.

Some of the 'fillers' have the added merit that they can be developed into more major investigations or are capable of being extended. Many of them are suitable for any age group.

I hope that by now, you, yourself, are enjoying playing with investigations from time to time and that your pupils are becoming familiar with the processes of mathematical thinking that enable them to explore and create their own mathematics.

The last word must go to a head of mathematics in the early 1960s, who realised that pupils who had their interest aroused and were allowed time to follow this interest in one lesson would work harder during the rest of the week. The Staff Inspector for Mathematics found this message on the school syllabus:

MASTERS ARE FORBIDDEN NOT TO WASTE TIME IN MATHEMATICS LESSONS.

Quickies

1 Multiplying pairs

$$
\begin{array}{cc}
24\times & 42\times \\
\underline{63} & \underline{36} \\
1512 & 1512
\end{array}
$$

(i) Choose other pairs of two-digit numbers
(ii) Investigate.

2 Consecutive numbers

Pick any two consecutive numbers and multiply them together. Repeat with different consecutive pairs. Is the answer even or odd?

Explain why.

What happens if you multiply three consecutive numbers? Or four consecutive numbers?

3 Hats

This hat is made from six pieces, each the same shape and size.

How many different hats can be made:
   (a) if three pieces are black and three are white?
   (b) if each piece can be either black or white?

4 Adders

Choose any three digits less than ten.
Make all the possible two-digit numbers with them.
Add all these two-digit numbers together.
Divide by the sum of your original three digits.
What is your answer?
Choose three other starting digits.

Try starting with four digits and make three-digit numbers.

5 **Stamps**
If you have only 3p and 5p stamps, what priced postage can you make up? Are there values which you cannot make up?

What if you have 4p and 6p stamps?
Are there values which you cannot make up?

Try other pairs of stamps.

6 **Calculator multiples**
What is the largest number you can make on your calculator using:

$\boxed{1}$ $\boxed{2}$ $\boxed{3}$ $\boxed{4}$ $\boxed{5}$ $\boxed{\times}$ and $\boxed{=}$?

How can you be sure?
Can you make a larger number if you also use $\boxed{\div}$ and $\boxed{\cdot}$?

7 **Walkabout**
Draw a square 3 by 3 grid. Start in one corner. Visit each square once and once only without making diagonal moves.

i.e. 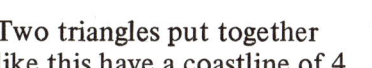 is OK   is not.

In how many different ways can you do this?
What about 4 by 4 grids?

8 **Four 4s**
How many numbers can you make using up to four 4s?
e.g. $1 = 4 \div 4$
and $2 = (4 + 4) \div 4$
(*Harder*) How many can you make using exactly four 4s?
e.g. $1 = \dfrac{(4 \times 4)}{(4 \times 4)}$

9 **Coastlines**
One equilateral triangle
is said to have a coastline of 3.

Two triangles put together
like this have a coastline of 4.

Put together like this
their coastline is 6.

What are the longest
and shortest coastlines
you can make with three, four, . . . triangles?

10 **Mathsnakes**
Mathsnake (1, 2, 3) does a wriggle on squared paper:
1 square forward and turn right,
2 squares forward and turn right,
3 squares forward and turn right.
Investigate its tracks made by consecutive wriggles.
Investigate other mathsnakes.

11 Intersections

Two straight lines can cut each other (intersect) at only one point. How many intersections can three lines have? Four lines? . . . .

12 How many halves?

Use dotty paper.
Here is one way to halve a 4 x 4 square.
How many other ways can you halve it?

13   More investigations

Problem 13.1
Symmetry

In how many ways can you place n stars so that there is at least one line of symmetry?
    (First define your problem!)

Problem 13.2
Cubes

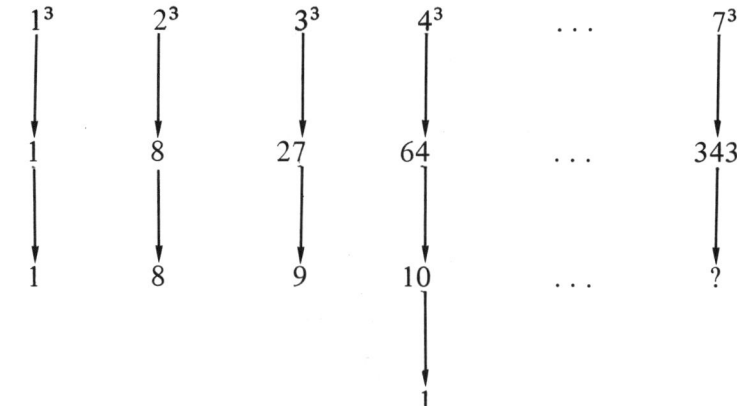

Investigate.

List of investigations